AF478397

Over the Great Navajo Trail

AMS PRESS

NEW YORK

Carl Eickemeyer

Over the Great Navajo Trail

By

Carl Eickemeyer

Author of "Among the Pueblo Indians." Life Member of the American Museum
of Natural History, New York. Member of the American Folk=Lore Society

Illustrated with Photographs
taken by the Author.......

New York, 1900

Library of Congress Cataloging in Publication Data

Eickemeyer, Carl.
    Over the great Navajo Trail.

    Reprint of the 1900 ed. published by the Press
of J. J. Little, New York.
    1.   Navaho Indians.   2.   Navaho Indian Reserva-
tions.   3.   New Mexico — Description and travel.
4.   Arizona — Description and travel.   I.   Title.
E99.N3E3   1976   970'.004'97   74-7965
ISBN 0-404-11853-4

From the edition of 1900, New York
First AMS edition published in 1976
Manufactured in the United States of America

AMS PRESS INC.
NEW YORK, N. Y. 10003

To

My Wife

Lilian Westcott Eickemeyer

Contents

Contents

V

List of Illustrations

Introduction

Introduction

N my book, " Among the Pueblo Indians," the kodak aided the manuscript to such an extent in portraying the strange and realistic scenes witnessed among these curiously interesting people, that it is my wish to use the same method in conveying the desired impression to the reader in the present instance.

With this object in view, therefore, I offer this volume, containing the photographs and an account of my experiences among a people who are yet in a state unaffected by the influences of civilization or by contact with white settlers; who will probably never, to any great extent, occupy the fertile valleys, few and far between the great barren wastes of the lava-capped mesas of New Mexico and Arizona.

The few square miles of mountainous country within the borders of the Navajo Reservation—the terminus

Introduction

of the Great Navajo Trail—are, with the exception of traders and the Indian Agent, seldom visited by whites. It is here the Indian is found in a perfectly natural state, living according to ancient customs and beliefs, and carrying on the industries he has followed for generations. Horse, cattle, and sheep raising, as well as the art of silversmithing, were undoubtedly acquired from the early Spanish settlers; while the weaving of beautifully designed blankets, an industry for which Navajo women are noted, is evidently traceable to the Aztecs.

Pottery-making, at which the Pueblo Indians excel, has never been developed by the Navajos beyond a crude, blackened, half-baked, round-bottomed clay jar, inartistic in shape, and without glaze or decoration. The art of basket-weaving is not carried on to any great extent by the Navajos.

The Navajos, although superstitious in the extreme, believing in witches and evil spirits of every description, are industrious, energetic, and, up to the limit their land allows, they are self-supporting. Some have even acquired considerable wealth by raising sheep, goats, and horses, which now number many thousands.

Any hatred the race may have for the whites seems

Introduction

to exist only in regard to the method of compulsory education in vogue, which deprives the Indian of his children—the greatest of all his possessions.

My mention of Navajo men and women as bucks and squaws, terms now questioned by literary critics, is merely to use words the Indians themselves use in speaking, not only of each other, but of men and women in general. Often in my travels have I heard the expression, " White man's squaw."

CARL EICKEMEYER

NOVEMBER, 1900.

1

The Great Navajo Trail

¶

The Great Navajo Trail

History of the Trail.—Reception of Early Settlers.—Early Skirmishes.—Condition during the Rebellion.—Navajos, Apaches, Comanches, and Kiowas.—Navajo Reservation.

IN travelling through rough and mountainous New Mexico, a section of country only partially settled by a people who at one time inhabited our land from the Atlantic to the Pacific Ocean, and from the Gulf far into the British possessions on the north; with their original manners, customs, and religion, and having a language of their own to which they still adhere; together with a people who are the descendants of the Spaniards, and yet speak a corruption of the mother tongue, without the slightest knowledge of the English language, one not accustomed to their ways, and living under entirely different circumstances, feels as if he were in a foreign country rather than within the borders of his native land; and he is naturally looked upon as an intruder.

It is not at all to be wondered at, therefore, that, during the early days of the invasion of New Mexico by the whites, they were looked upon with contempt by the Indians and Mexicans, who with the exception of a few, threw every obstruction possible in the way of those who had come from the far East, over unbeaten trails, to make this country their home.

The Mexicans, living in little adobe settlements along river beds, whose streams furnished water enough to irrigate their fields in the spring, and were dry during the remainder of the year, when the only water supply was from alkali springs bubbling up not far from the river beds, were continually at war with the Indians—each retaliating for some former raid of the other, when their homes had been burned and their cattle driven off. These depredations were gradually transforming an industrious, home-loving people into hostile bands.

With these and other uncertainties the settlers had

to contend when the War of the Rebellion broke out, making another division in sentiment which had to adjust itself. There was the Confederate army in Texas to cope with; the liability of an insurrection among the Mexicans; and the continual raids of the Navajos and Apaches on the west of the Rio Grande, and the Comanches and Kiowas on the east.

To pursue the Indians over arid plains and through mountain passes, where animal life, with the exception of gophers, lizards, and rattlesnakes, cannot exist, was a hazardous attempt for a company of cavalry, and an impossibility for infantry, who, in many cases, became demoralized while advancing to the front, their gallant leaders having been picked off, victims of an unseen foe, who were fighting from rock to rock, making every shot tell. From these experiences, it was soon found that the only tactics to be used against such skirmishing were to adopt a similar course, more accordant to the methods used by the old Indian fighters present, who had exercised this mode of warfare from the time of their early arrival in the country.

The Mexicans, who could take some ears of corn and a few tortillas, and start across country on their ponies, travelling for days without water, were much more feared by the Indians than were the United States troops, who, being strained to their utmost by the invasion of the country by the Texans, were not always able to keep the roving Indians in subjection.

The inhabitants of the country were thus kept in a constant state of excitement, and it was for the safety of all that the United States Government sought the best method of quelling these disturbances—namely, the removal of the Indians to reservations, where they might settle down in permanent homes, isolated from the other inhabitants of New Mexico. This was not accomplished until near the close of the Rebellion, when Col. Kit Carson, at the head of the Navajo Expedition, succeeded, with much difficulty and hard fighting, in placing the Navajos, band after band, at Bosque Redondo on the Pecos Rio, near old Fort Sumner, where they were kept prisoners of war until a treaty of peace was signed. This tract of land proved too small for the 7,000 Navajos encamped there, in consequence of which, in a destitute condition, they were removed to their present reservation.

The Navajo Reservation, containing over 12,000 square miles, lies in the northwestern corner of New Mexico and the northeastern part of Arizona, and at the present time has a population of about 20,000. In the early days of its history, the trails leading to and from the reservation were formed not only by the wagon trains that brought supplies to the troops and the Indian Agent, but by the Indians, who, in many instances, with all their possessions—a few blankets, bows, and arrows, and old guns—would go to the border towns and trade these for one or two sheep, which formed the nucleus that was the foundation of future prosperity. The great Navajo trail, which has opened the way between the reservation and the Rio Grande, is the path over which the Navajos have for years driven their bunches of horses and cattle to the Indian pueblos, where they traded them, generally for bead-work, for which the Pueblos are noted.

That part of the trail lying between Santa Fé and Gallup forms part of the old Santa Fé trail, which was the southern of the two principal routes between Leavenworth, Kansas, and San Francisco, taken by the emigrants and early settlers who wended their way over this desolate trail from eastern Kansas in search of fortune, after the discovery of gold in California in 1848.

The northern route was over the Great Salt Lake

trail, through Denver, Fort Laramie, Salt Lake City, and Carson City to California. Each route was equally hard to travel, the Santa Fé trail avoiding the rugged mountains to the north, only to substitute the arid deserts of New Mexico and Arizona, where many perished from want of water.

Previous to the building of the Union Pacific Railroad in 1869, these trails formed the old mail-stage routes (when passengers and mail and express matter occupied the same quarters), as well as being the road over which many thousand emigrants travelled in their prairie schooners to form the early population of California. And over these trails, the greater part of the provisions consumed by these pioneer settlers was transported by wagon trains of from ten to thirty wagons, each drawn by six yoke of oxen, hauling fifty hundredweight—the wagons themselves weighing fifteen hundred pounds each. The time consumed in these trips from the Missouri to the Pacific varied from three to four months.

The trail between Santa Fé and the pueblo of Zuñi was followed by Coronado as early as 1542 ; while that part between the Missouri and Santa Fé was opened in 1805 (improved in 1844 by the United

The Great Navajo Trail

States Government under the direction of Col. Kit Carson), and was continually travelled until 1878, when the Santa Fé Railroad was built, practically over the line of the old trail, which then fell into disuse, and which will, in time, be entirely obliterated.

To-day, after years of neglect, the road shows the effect of heavy rains that have washed out the soil in the rocky acclivities, leaving bare ledges of rock, at the foot of which are bowlders of lava obstructing the roadway. Near the river beds the strong whirlwinds have picked up the sand and deposited it in drifts, which offer such resistance to the wagon that travelling is much more difficult than formerly.

In order that one may see that part of our great Western country which is yet in a condition unaffected by the advancement of civilization, he must follow the trails and rough roads for miles, and endure hardships that are to be experienced only when travelling at great distances from the railroad.

11

Starting Over the Trail

¶

Starting Over the Trail

Leaving Santa Fé.—Prairie-dog Villages.—Physical Characteristics of the Country.—Jemez Pueblo.—Sleeping with One Eye Open.—United States Troops.— Meeting Navajos.—Cabezon Peak.

DURING my visits to the Indian pueblos of New Mexico, I became greatly interested in the Navajos, many of whom had come across the country from their reservation, to be present at the dances of the Pueblos, and to trade their beautifully-woven blankets and their silver-work with these Indians. Their stern features and fine physiques, due to the natural life they lead, together with their skill in handling horses, led me to choose the Navajo country as the objective point of my next outing.

In the summer of 1896, in company with my wife and Sam, an Indian interpreter, I left Santa Fé to travel westward over the Great Navajo Trail, with a saddle pony, team, and a wagon loaded with the necessary articles of camp life. The name given Sam at the Agency school was Sam Reader, while his Navajo name was De-not-sosa, meaning Rope. The morning was bright and beautiful, the sky cloudless, and a clear, cool breeze from the southwest made life on the road full of enjoyment. In the distance loomed up great mountains—our landmarks, which we would not reach for several days. Back over the gradually-rising prairie, lay Santa Fé at the foot of the gray-topped mountains, until, in the growing distance, it became smaller and smaller—then vanished.

We passed many ox-teams leisurely drawing loads of hay which the Mexicans from Agua Fria were taking to their corrals to store as winter food for their cattle. In many cases where one team closely followed another, the driver of the second was perched on the load of the former, evidently for

MEXICAN OX-TEAMS

STARTING OVER THE TRAIL

companionship, while the oxen trudged sleepily along behind, stopping only when the front team halted.

The prairie was here and there dotted with prairie-dog villages, some of the inhabitants of which were sitting on their haunches near their burrows—others were running around, gathering roots. A burrowing owl—a small brownish-mottled bird—was standing erectly on the edge of a deserted prairie-dog burrow, inquisitively eying the passer-by. Upon being approached, he was not in the least alarmed; while his companions, the prairie dogs, slid down their burrows at the first sight of the strangers.

These owls are common throughout the West and Southwest. They take deserted burrows of prairie-dog villages for their homes, possibly on account of the facility thus offered for obtaining mice and insects, upon which they chiefly subsist.

The Cerrillos Mountains, surrounded by conically-shaped hills, rise from the lower end of the plain. These mountains are noted for their rich mineral resources, containing mines of gold and silver and of turquoise, which, before the arrival of the Spaniards, were worked by the Pueblo Indians, who to-day have bits of turquoise in their strings of beads, and are excellent judges of its quality.

To the right of the plain extends a high wall of sand rising in a steep slope, topped off with a layer of lava, and forming a barrier, along the side of which flows the Rio Santa Fé. In the distance the road climbs the sandy slope like a white chalk-mark, cutting through the dark edge of the lava to the top of the mesa. For miles the road is level, except for the gradual undulations of the prairie, and we were able to jog along at a good rate of speed—the team in their steady gait, the saddle pony in his fox-trot, pegging away over the road with an air of contentment as if his task were an everyday occurrence. The monotony was relieved now and then by Sam, who, when tired of cracking the whip, broke into a chant—one of those sung by the Indians in their dances and festivals, and which have been handed down, with but little change or variation, from generation to generation.

Many shore-larks were seen along the road. As we neared them, some of the males raised their little horned heads, gracefully displaying the black crescents on their breasts, as if inquiring whether it were necessary to flutter further along out of danger. This lark is decidedly a ground bird, living on insects and seeds, and never alighting on trees or shrubs. This characteristic, together with its never having to grasp its food, is undoubtedly the cause of the peculiar growth of the single rear toe-claw, which grows straight to the rear, needle-shaped, about half an inch long. The three front toe-claws are only slightly curved.

Passing a bunch of cattle grazing not far from the trail, and tended by two Mexicans, we reached the edge of the mesa, where the road, becoming very rough, descends through deep passes around the edge of the cliff known as La Bajada. Here and there, large bowlders, laid bare by denudation, had rolled to the foot of the slope, which, together with the deep gullies in the road, made it necessary to tie up both back wheels of the wagon, as a brake, under such circumstances, is of little use.

At sunset we reached the plain below and camped beside a stream which runs down the deep cañon cut in the mesa from which we had just descended. Across the stream lay a little adobe village, with its fields of corn and alfalfa extending from the hillside to the river-bed. As the sun was sinking behind the distant mountains, shedding a soft light over the country, the little square windows in the adobe huts of the Mexicans emitted rays of candlelight—as if in imitation of the heavens, where star after star lighted up the clear blue sky, making the black line of the mountains clearly discernible against the horizon.

The bed in the tent being ready, we turned in between blankets spread on a wagon-cover on the ground, and, with a saddle for a pillow, settled ourselves for a good night's rest; while Sam, rolling himself in his blanket, slept in the bottom of the wagon, with a gun under his coat (that served as a pillow), avowing that no one ever stole up on a camp where he slept.

The horses, which had been picketed out in front of the tent, now and then broke the stillness of the night by pulling buffalo grass, and snorting at intervals. A coyote, seeing our camp, came to the top of the nearest knoll, and, with his nose pointed to the sky, gave his laughing bark. This unearthly cry startled the dogs in the village. On being aroused, a general fight began, probably started by a dog that had been too inquisitive as to the whereabouts of the coyote, and had wandered into a different part of the town, where other dogs took hold of him by mistake, and

EDGE OF A LAVA-CAPPED MESA

the growling, barking, and yelping could all be heard at one time.

The dogs of these villages, from their build and color, appear to be part wolf or coyote, being tall, thin, and shaggy, and having small heads, thick necks, and deep chests.

For a while all was quiet, except for the continual noise of the horses pulling the grass, until the braying of a burro, in its two-note call, was heard, and, in turn, answered by another from a different part of the corral. The night passed, with slumbers broken, off and on, until the starlight grew dim, and the sun began to light up the plain, letting us know it was time to start the fire, and put on the old blackened coffee-pot, the one object of all others sacred in the eyes of the camper. As we rose from our bed on the ground, a centipede ran swiftly in and out among the blankets, and in trying to catch him we came across a scorpion, nestling in one corner of the bed, as if lazily waiting for his breakfast. He, as well as the centipede, was put in alcohol with some other specimens we had collected, and another day's journey began.

The cañon of the Rio Grande, its sides streaked with white sandstone, from which it derives its name of White Rock Cañon, here ends, and the country spreads out into a fertile plain. The tall, spreading cottonwood trees along the sides of the stream are the first indications of water the traveller perceives when crossing these broad plains ; and he knows he is nearing a settlement. A Mexican town, most likely, with its five or six adobe houses, its church, without which no Mexican village is complete, and the priest who, in addition to his other duties, forgives the sins of the Mexicans ; and, judging from their sinning propensities, he must be kept busy.

The priest is the one person of importance in a Mexican town, inspiring the people with nearly as much awe as does the United States revenue officer, who frequently visits the towns to see that the government stamp is on the whiskey barrels. His place is nicely laid out with flower gardens and fruit trees ; his cattle and horses always look in the finest condition ; and he has the best the land affords. Altogether, his lot is a pleasant one.

Near the Rio Grande the road is lined on both sides by cottonwood trees, which, for a short distance, protect one from the intense heat of the sun. Crossing the marshes, spotted here and there with patches of

FORDING THE RIO GRANDE

alkali, resembling frost, we reached the river, where, although the water was up to the horses' bellies, it was not too deep to ford with the wagon. One of the greatest dangers encountered in travelling across this country with an outfit is in fording the streams, which, at the time the snow is melting in the mountains, and during the rainy seasons, carry down large quantities of water. The river-beds contain many quicksand holes, and when fording a place at one time a team may cross in safety, while two hours later the bed will have been washed out to a depth of six or eight feet. It is here the saddle pony is of the greatest use. He advances carefully, step by step, should the ground near the stream be soft, satisfying himself that the river-bed is reasonably hard before crossing. In this way, one finds the fords, and crosses with his team, not running any risk of having his provisions washed down the stream.

We camped a mile from the river, far enough up the slope, we thought, to be out of range of the gnats and mosquitoes; but they followed us in great swarms, evidently considering the change of diet from Mexican to American an agreeable one. It was not until a smudge of green cedar had been built in the tent that we were at all comfortable, and even then the insects did not entirely disappear.

Next day we engaged a team to help us over the mesa to Jemez, an Indian pueblo, with a population of about four hundred, situated on the east side of the Rio Jemez. The road over the divide is heavy, and, as the Jemez gives the next water supply, the journey of forty-two miles should be made in a day. The young Mexican from whom we had hired the horses agreed to come to camp with his team the following morning, and at sunrise he turned up with them, such as they were. After fixing his old harness with rope, and his crude-looking whiffletree with hay-wire, we put his team in the lead, and started out to ascend the Mesa of Santa Ana.

We drove through thickly-wooded groves of red and white cedar, crossing one hill after another, until, from the bed of the last arroyo, we ascended one of the mesas that are characteristic of the scenery of the great central plateau from which the Rocky Mountains rise. They spread out for miles on either side of mountain ranges, which contain the craters of extinct volcanoes, that at one time poured forth the lava which forms the tops of the surrounding table-

A BIT OF ROUGH ROAD

lands. These mesas are cut by deep cañons, which were formed at a time when a greater amount of water than there is to-day was carried down the slopes; when torrents from cloudbursts, flowing in rapid succession during the rainy seasons, wore through the lava and washed out the underlying sand, leaving perpendicular cliffs and pinnacles, which are counter-worn by the high winds of to-day.

By the roadside are scrub cedar, amola, and buffalo grass a foot high, growing out of the hot sand, which, as the sun beats down upon it, brings on an unbearable thirst to the traveller as he goes on, mile after mile, over the arid plain.

In decided contrast to the nights, which in this country are uncomfortably cold, so intense is the noonday heat that one often finds it impossible to rest his hand on the pommel of his saddle. Among the few forms of animal life existing under these circumstances is the prairie rattlesnake, seen from time to time along the road; his slumbers being temporarily disturbed by the passer-by, he rattles his defiance and crawls away over the burning sands.

Suddenly the country changes; becomes broken up by sand hills, bounded by rugged cliffs with bright coloring of red and white sandstone, blended with the colors, in the strata, of blue and green limestone. To the northwest is the deep, black cañon of the Guadalupe, joining that of the Rio Jemez. These cañons cut deeply into the vast, sweeping mesas, until high, barren-topped mountains form their boundary against the horizon.

We camped on the outskirts of Jemez pueblo, where a strong wind, sweeping up the river-bed with great force, picked up the sand like so much chaff, making it almost impossible to put the tent in position, and pulling out the stakes as fast as they could be driven. Waiting for a cessation in the blow, we drove the stakes and piled enough sand on the side canvas to keep the tent in position.

The Mexican who had helped us over the mesa to Jemez sat watching us get supper. He could not, it seemed, make up his mind whether to stay in camp with us, or to sleep in a corral across the river. He said at first he would start for home in the early morning, when the moon came up; then he changed his mind and said: "At sunrise I will go." Not knowing when he would pass our camp, and thinking he might try to increase his day's earnings to the value of one of

A PRAIRIE FOUR-IN-HAND

our horses, we tied them to the wagon, and slept, as is customary in this part of the country, with one eye open.

At sunrise we were awakened by the chant of an Indian who was tending a bunch of cayuses (Indian ponies) in the hills a short distance from camp. The sounds floated into the tent through the still morning air, then died away in the distance as the singer went on his way over the hills. Soon the town was astir, and smoke could be seen coming from chimney after chimney as breakfast was being prepared in the little houses. It was a picturesque sight—the Indians collecting around our camp. They had espied it from the village, and one by one they sauntered up to satisfy their curiosity concerning the strangers. There were scantily-clad children with those still younger on their backs, who looked as if they needed more protection from the cold winds of the early morning than the little cotton slips they wore. Buxom girls in their beads and finery, and stalwart youths, crowded around the fire. Mothers and fathers of the little ones were there, and even those whose whitened locks told of approaching old age were among the number.

Suddenly the attention of the crowd was turned toward the river-bed, where several wagon trains could be seen coming toward us. The Indians, on perceiving them, ran to the roadside. As the company drew nearer we recognized two troops of cavalry mounted on large black horses. Each soldier wore the regulation uniform of blue, a broad-brimmed hat, and, with a carbine swinging from the right side of the saddle, appeared as if ready for business should occasion require. They had come over the trail from Fort Wingate, the military reservation, where they are stationed, in readiness to answer to a call from the surrounding country. Each company was followed by its ambulance and heavy pack mules, who showed their strength at every step, as they carried their heavy loads over the deep sand of the river-bed. Far in the rear, like a small white dot, was the provision wagon drawn by six mules, and guarded by ten or twelve of the troopers, who looked as if they could protect their charge against any band that might chance to hold them up. The Indians in the pueblo gathered on the housetops and watched in silence the procession march through their little town ; then they returned to work.

Three miles south of Jemez is San Ysidro, a Mexi-

UNITED STATES CAVALRY

can town with a small population, who lead the uneventful, easy-going life characteristic of the race. In
point of industrial achievement, however, San Ysidro
is in advance of the average Mexican settlement. The
little blacksmith shop, where wagons are repaired,
horse-shoeing being a rare occurrence, was certainly a
novelty in this part of the country; while the primi-
tive mill near by, whose stone derived its power from
a vertically-mounted turbine, was unique in the extreme, and would, no doubt, excite the interest of
some of the engineers of the Niagara Falls power
companies.

Just out of the town are many sparkling alkali
springs. These look very inviting to the thirsty traveller; but one swallow would cause him much suffering
and greater thirst, as the water nearly tans the tongues
and mouths of those who drink it. Cattle in the
vicinity occasionally drink the water in small quantities without any noticeable ill effects, while those
from other sections, drinking it for the first time, are
prostrated.

Across Salt Creek, the narrow cañon we entered
forms a picturesque and romantic guide for the road.
Perpendicular ledges of rock extend on either side to

a height of two hundred feet, and in the rugged cliffs were perched, here and there, brown eagles.

At the end of the cañon the road ascends very abruptly to the divide. Here it was that three Navajos rode up, keeping by our side for some distance. They had just traded their last horse at the pueblos along the Rio Grande, and were returning home, their pockets filled with silver and beads, the proceeds of the trade. When they passed on ahead, our team being unable to keep pace with their horses, we noticed that one of the three always kept his eyes in our direction. When he tired another turned in his saddle, and so on, until they disappeared over the ridge. They evidently feared we might hold them up from behind, not an uncommon trick of the Mexicans; and, as they carried with them the proceeds of their year's labor, they would take no chances.

A steep, rocky hill leads to the top of the next divide, and here the saddle pony again proved his usefulness by helping the team draw the heavy load to the top of the hill. A half-hitch was put in the pommel of his saddle, and, with the other end of the rope attached to the pole of the wagon, he pulled, with all his strength, until we reached the summit.

Starting Over the Trail

Twenty miles westward stands Cabezon Peak, in the broad valley of the Puerco. High mountains all around break up the plains; and in deep cañons, often at a depth of two thousand feet, run streams which for ages have cut their way through the thick layers of lava, sandstone, and clays, forming perpendicular cliffs, precipices, and buttes, worn by the exposure to the heavy rains and winds until they resemble ruined castles and cities.

As we neared Cabezon Peak, it seemed to stand out like a monument of ebony, in the changing light of the setting sun; and, in striking contrast to the background of eroded cliffs and buttes, it formed a picture at once so vivid and beautiful that we gazed silently at the grandeur of the sight.

Nothing is more impressive, when travelling through this lonely country, when the sun is sinking to rest, than to come upon a single grave by the wayside, but a few feet from the trail, where some poor fellow, who has died from exposure or want of water, lies buried. Far from any settlement, away from home and friends, he lies alone; the little wooden cross, with its Spanish inscription, being a touching tribute to his memory.

III

Cabezon and Westward

Ⅲ

Cabezon and Westward

Cabezon.—Frontier Whiskey.—Indian Ponies.—San Mateo.—Mexican Cattle-raising.—New Mexican Politics.—Pueblo Ruins.—The Penitente.—The Continental Divide.

NORTHWEST of Cabezon Peak lies the town of Cabezon, with its one-story adobe houses, its little church, a store, and one saloon. The population is entirely Mexican, with the exception of a white man who runs the village store and trades his wares with the Indians for articles of their manufacture.

We entered Cabezon about noon, and, as our stock of provisions needed replenishing, we drove up to the little store, followed by several

Mexicans, who had escorted us from the outskirts of the town. The store is the regular general store of the western Mexican villages, well supplied with groceries, drygoods, hardware, harness, and grain; and, in addition to his other duties, the storekeeper is postmaster of the place, from which the mail goes out once a week to the nearest railroad town.

There was the usual array of shooting irons behind the counter, better, by far, than a watchdog. From the rafters hung coffee-pots, frying-pans, pails, sheep-shears, etc. In one corner, at the end of the long counter, was a pile of rifles and carbines, some in their buckskin-fringed cases, having been traded by the Indians for provisions, at times when their crops failed to yield a sufficient livelihood, and when provisions were of more value to them than were their guns. The stocks of some were bound with rawhide to keep them together; while others, in a better state of preservation, were ornamented with brass-headed tacks, and engraved with the private marks of their former owners. Some had been fired so many times that the rifling was entirely worn away.

A lot of idle Mexicans had collected around the place, apparently with no motive other than to have a good rest (this seems characteristic of the race),

COMING UP THE RIVER-BED

and to satisfy their curiosity; for when a stranger appears in their midst they are all attention—leaving, for a few moments, the support of the counter, and becoming, for the time, really animated as they start in to catechize him. They watch his every step; look over his outfit; inquire the whereabouts of his camp; whether his horses are tired—this last not to be of assistance in case one needs a lift, but merely out of curiosity. They ask where he is going, and whence he comes. While we were going through this customary examination, a young fellow rode rapidly up, having spurred his ill-fed horse into a run. In front of the store he pulled him up short, with the aid of a Mexican bit, and dismounted, much to the enjoyment of those sitting around the door. He had evidently heard there were strangers in the town, and had hastened to the store to be present at the general inspection.

It was here we saw the first Navajos in any great numbers. Many of them were wandering through the streets, and standing around the corrals, looking after their horses. Here and there, squaws rode along, sitting astride in perfectly natural positions in their saddles; for in Indian equestrian circles the side-saddle is unknown, a woman often riding forty miles a day with ease and without fatigue. Some had large rolls of blankets, which they had just finished, and were taking them to the store to trade for provisions.

On a hilltop overlooking the town was an encampment of seven Navajos, who were out on a horse-selling expedition. They were reclining against their saddles, that had been thrown on the ground at the head of their temporary beds, which they had made by hollowing out the sand and spreading their saddle-blankets thereon. Near by sat a young fellow, stripped to the waist in the cool breeze, mending with sinew his shirt, which he had torn while riding through the brush after a horse that had strayed from the bunch.

Sam at once joined them, and inquired as to the prospects of getting water and the condition of the grass on the road to San Mateo, our next stopping-place. He asked also the price of a saddle one of the men was leaning against. At this the expressions on their faces changed to serious ones. The leader refused to have the saddle examined, and told Sam something in Navajo, which he interpreted: " He no sell ; he need saddle to go home." We were not long

THE AMBULANCE

deceived by this sophistry, however, the real reason being too apparent. Under each saddle was a bottle of whiskey, and they wanted to take no chances of falling in with a Government spy, who would deprive them of their much-cherished treasure.

The Indians are very fond of white-man's whiskey, as they call it. This is not surprising, considering the exposure they have to endure, as in the coldest weather they are very lightly clad. Their apparel consists generally of a shirt open down the front, leaving the chest exposed; a breechcloth, leggins, and moccasins. Over these thin garments a blanket carelessly is thrown, making a most picturesque object of the wearer. Their heads are usually encircled by a handkerchief, in which is rolled up a little money, tobacco, buttons, sinew, or other small possessions.

The Indians' method of obtaining their toddy from the storekeepers is to give a Mexican some money with which to buy the article. The Mexican is then given his choice of half the money or half the whiskey, which tastes like a combination of kerosene oil and tobacco, and it is not at all to be wondered at that white-man's whiskey makes the Indian crazy.

The bunch of ponies, or cayuses, in the village

corral near by had been brought in to sell to the Mexicans. They were all fine saddle ponies, only half broken. These horses sometimes develop queer traits in their training. What is known as "busting a bronco" is not practised among the Indians. If a horse bucks when the saddle is put on him a rope with a slipknot on it is put around his neck and he is choked down. During the treatment he thus receives in being thrown one would think his end had come; but, his air supply being cut off, he soon has enough bucking, and what little he does afterward is not at the expense of the rider. These ponies are as sure-footed as the mountain sheep, going up and down the nearly perpendicular sides of a cañon without a slip. They are typical cow-ponies, and, when broken, understand the art of driving cattle as well as do their riders. They are careful where they step, cleverly avoiding soft ground and gopher burrows; and when settling down to a fox-trot they can travel from sunrise to sunset over the roughest stretch of unbroken country, where the sand covers their hoofs at every step. When striking the rocks of the mountains they can carry their riders or packs, whichever the case may be, with ease and safety, and when reaching a

BLACKSMITH SHOP

deep ford they can swim in the swiftest current. When a wagon is stranded, and the team unable to start, the pony is ready to help; and when a half-hitch is put on the pommel of his saddle, and the other end of the rope is attached to the pole of the wagon, he will pull until the cinches break or something moves. He is always well, and seems to enjoy his experiences, whether ridden by a tenderfoot around a summer resort, or when aiding in the "killins" (shooting scrapes) of the cowboys over their stolen cattle. If his rider stays in the saddle on a cold morning, which is usually begun with a spell of bucking, the pony is satisfied to settle down to work. He can kick his way out of any bunch of Eastern horses in which he might be placed, and, unlike the latter, who would starve under similar circumstances, when turned loose in winter he can make his living by rustling for grass through the deep snow.

Early next morning, as the heavy mist was rising from the mountain passes to the north—like a ghost which, having performed its mission, vanishes before the morning sunlight—we broke camp, and, with our blankets still around us, turned westward toward Willow Springs against a wind that penetrated to the bone.

Near the road, a band of Navajos was encamped, huddling together around the camp-fire, the flames of which were blown nearly horizontal by the keen wind, which caused them to pull their blankets more tightly around them. Through the country were many Navajo farms, with their small patches of Indian corn and their corrals full of sheep and goats.

Far in the distance rose Mount Taylor (or San Mateo), a now extinct volcano. San Mateo (Sacred Mountain) is eleven thousand, three hundred and eighty-nine feet above sea-level, and is of black lava, of which many of the mountains in the vicinity are formed. In San Mateo, according to Navajo mythology, dwelt, many years ago, the giant Yeitso, clothed in armor, and a special terror to all who came within his realm. Two Navajo boys (twins) were travelling through the country, alone, in search of their father, so goes the legend. They met the Sun, who told them of Yeitso and how they could slay the monster while he was drinking at the spring of Tho satho. The Sun further told the boys he would help them by knocking off the giant's armor with a great thunderbolt. When they reached the spring, they saw the giant stooping over it, drinking. Yeitso, on perceiving

THE MILL

them, hurled a thunderbolt at them; but, seeing it coming, they dropped to the ground, and it passed over them. Every one of the giant's missiles was thus evaded, until he had no more; then the promised bolt came down from the Sun and rent his armor, and the boys fell on the naked giant and cut him to pieces. They cut off his head, and hurled it a distance, when it was transformed into a hill, which stands to this day, and is known as El Cabezon, the peak we had passed but the day before. The great torrent of blood that flowed coagulated into black rock, and can still be seen on the tops of the mesas around San Mateo. This legend can be found in full among the works of Dr. Washington Matthews, and a perusal of it will well repay the reader.

When we camped for dinner, an old Mexican, riding over the plain, reined in his horse as he reached our camp, and dismounted. He took the saddle from the pony, and, putting a pair of rawhide hobbles on him, turned him loose to graze. The man sat watching us until what seemed to him, no doubt, an elaborate meal was prepared, and he told us the experience that was the cause of his journey over the mesa. His boy, it seemed, had been tending a herd of sheep and goats in the hills, and when he returned after a lapse of two weeks, tired, footsore, and hungry, and without the sheep, the father found he had been attacked by three Mexicans, who, after trying unsuccessfully to kill the boy, had stolen some of his sheep as he retreated amid a volley of bullets, which, fortunately, went wide of the mark. From a distance he could see the men kill, first his dog, then seven or eight of his flock, and, packing the carcasses of the sheep on their ponies, ride off in the direction of Guadalupe, a small town about five miles south of Cabezon. The remainder of the sheep—the boy being too frightened to return to them—were left alone, at the mercy of the wolves and coyotes, who are continually on the watch for a herd; and even when an attendant is near they sometimes catch a sick young one too weak to keep up with the rest of the flock.

We shared our dinner with the old man, who seemed to prefer it to the hard, dry tortillas he carried in an old flour-sack tied on the back of his saddle; and when Sam handed him a piece of watermelon, which the Indians of Jemez raise in great quantities, he looked pleased beyond description, as he said: "Bueno sandia" (good watermelon) and fell to eating

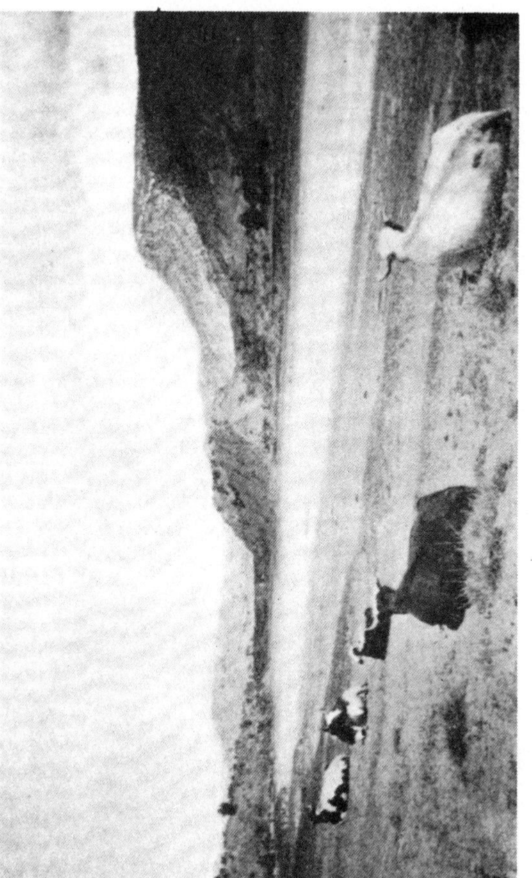

SALT CREEK

it. When he finished, he stepped behind his horse, that had just been saddled, and rubbed the rind over his head and face, seeming to enjoy the luxury of a good wash. This novel ablution was, from all appearances, the first the man had had for some time. As he threw the rind away, with an air of satisfaction he mounted his horse, and, with a "Gracias!" for what he had received, spurred the pony with the single spur he wore, and rode off.

One of the principal occupations of the people in this section of country is cattle-raising, and the appearance of the typical Mexican cowboy, driving his bunch of thin, wiry cattle along the road, on their way to and from the grazing land, where he carefully watches them, is not an uncommon sight. No cattle roam at large over the country here, as they do on the plains of Colorado and Texas; and the round-up is unknown. The reason for this can readily be seen, when, in a bunch of several hundred cattle the Mexican is watching, there may be seen sixty or seventy different brands, representing as many ranches in different parts of the country.

Cattle-stealing among the Mexicans is as common as cattle-raising among the Texans; and it is here the sheriffs and their faithful deputies are kept busy ferreting out the whereabouts of the principals of the "killins," which occur as a preventive in securing evidence against these young herders, who, being over-ambitious, have not the patience to allow their stock to increase by honest means. With these cattle-thieves, no chances can be taken; one must act quickly in dealing with them, or he will, in all probability, "bite the dust," and his bones be left to bleach on the prairie sand.

Among those who are constantly looking up these desperate characters is Thomas H. Tucker, a deputy sheriff of Santa Fé. Tom was thoroughly fitted for the work he is now doing by his experience in past years among the cattle-rustlers in Texas, where I first met him in all the glory of a cowboy's existence. His life has been an eventful one. When but twenty years of age, while on a visit to some friends in southern Arizona, the famous "Good War" between the cattle and sheep men began. These quarrels arise from the pasturing of sheep on the cattle-ranges. The sheep eat the grass down to the roots, so that, when the hot sun strikes it, it is burned beyond recovery, thus ruining the land for the pasture of cattle. Quarrels of this kind often occur, but are seldom

IN AN ARROYO

brought to the height of this war. Disinterested from any personal standpoint, save sympathy for his friends, Tom entered into the fight with all the enthusiasm of youthful vigor. It was here he was wounded in one of the skirmishes and given up for dead by his friends; but, rallying sufficiently to crawl three-quarters of a mile to the nearest ranch, he began to recover.

On returning to Texas, he took up ranching in the western section, where a man's existence depends largely on his quickness with the gun, in protecting his cattle against thieves, who start up in the Pan Handle, and drive their cattle, numbering two or three head, across the corner of New Mexico, picking up cattle from different ranches along the way. With their increased herds, they then make their way to the favorite watering-place in the Hueco Mountains, where, before they can add more to their enormous bunches, they meet their fate at the hands of Tom and his partners, who have done more to break up this lawless pursuit than any other ranchers in the country.

It was from this life he was called to Santa Fé, when, on the night of May 29, 1892, the sheriff, Frank Chavez, was shot to death by a group of Mexicans—members of the famous " Button Gang "—who were lying in wait for him in the shadow of the Church of San Rosario, not far from the centre of the town. This atrocious murder was the outcome of political differences which arise in consequence of the vicious and degraded methods practised by the prominent leaders of both parties.

The " Button Gang " consisted mostly of Mexicans, organized under the direct leadership of one of the influential Republicans, in opposition to the will of a Democratic secret society, known as the "White-Caps," and formed for a similar purpose. These societies satisfied political ambitions through perjury, forgery, embezzlement, and murder, and protected fellow criminals from imprisonment and the horror of the gallows to an extent found only in the Territory of New Mexico.

Such was the state of affairs when Governor Thornton took office in 1893, and he appointed William P. Cunningham sheriff, who, with Tom and Juan Otero as deputies, began to hunt for evidence against, and a " round-up " of, the " Button Gang " murderers. After killing Hipolito Virgil, a member of the executive committee of the gang, as well as being chief of police, coroner, and school commissioner of Santa Fé, the other principal desperadoes were captured ; and, after a long

IN THE CAÑON

trial which reeked with dishonesty and perjury, they were finally hanged. Thus ended the reign of terror. In clearing up the case, the people of Santa Fé are greatly indebted to the sheriff and his deputies for their faithful work, and the way in which they handled those outlaws, who, Tom avows, have no fear of a prison life; "but," he remarked, in relating this experience, "they don't like to be hung."

Late in the afternoon we reached San Mateo, and camped on the outskirts of the town. The night, although not unusual in this country, where, before morning, it invariably becomes cold, was very unpleasant. It began raining during the afternoon, as we were plodding along over the country, the horses slipping at every step; the large drops of rain transformed the fairly good road into one of slippery clay. From camp we could see a heavy cloudburst slowly approaching from the mountains east of us. Soon it was raining in the cornfields a short distance away, and when the wind, coming up stronger, lifted the heavy black clouds over our heads, the rain fell in torrents. The trenches we had previously dug around the tent, however, guided the water off as fast as it came down the side canvas, leaving the blankets dry. The night was damp and cold, and to sleep was almost impossible. Any one who has camped under such circumstances, sleeping on the ground with a stream of water running along each side of the bed, can well recall his experience, when the tent is wet through, the wood too wet to burn, and the wait for the morning sun a long and tedious one. Next morning was bright and clear, and the sun, shining in uninterrupted splendor upon the surrounding hills, soon warmed the atmosphere, and dried up the drenched country.

Very early two little Mexican girls came to camp, carrying an old tin pail between them. They stood watching me light the fire, a mystified expression on their faces, as they said : " The Señora ! " At this unusual call the Señora, who had not yet arisen, put her head out of the tent door and welcomed her little guests, who, it seemed, had no part of their greeting for me—it was all for the Señora. They had seen us drive through their town the night before, and had brought us a pail of sour milk. Our breakfast pancakes, or tortillas, as Sam called them, were thus an assured success, and a great improvement over those we usually mixed with water.

The little girls remained in camp most of the day,

A STOP FOR DINNER

trying to be of assistance to us where they could. At first we could not imagine what so attracted them to the spot; but the reason soon became evident from their conversation and actions. " Bonita Señora ! " said one. " Si," said the other, as she drew near the object of their admiration and stroked her hand. " Beautiful lady ! " A compliment out of the wilds of New Mexico.

It seems any one having blue eyes and a light complexion is considered beautiful by Mexican women, who, on Sundays and holidays, powder their dark faces until they are perfectly white; then, when decorated in their best attire of dark-colored calico, with their heads covered with black shawls, making a striking contrast to their ghastly faces, they repair to the little adobe church and worship, while the priest says mass beside the crudely-made altar and the images of their saints.

North of San Mateo are the ruins of a pueblo like many others scattered throughout the Navajo country, which, many years ago, was the home of the Pueblo Indians. These villages were probably abandoned on account of the scarcity of water, which caused an insufficient food supply for the subsistence of the increasing numbers. This accounts for the many pueblo ruins scattered throughout this barren region ; the removal of the Indians to the fertile valley of the Rio Grande being a necessity for the perpetuation of the race. Many of these ruins are still in a very fair state of preservation, several houses being still intact.

The Penitentes—that sacrifice-loving, self-torturing order of Franciscan Friars—are found at the height of their horrible practices at the little Mexican town of San Mateo, where, as at Taos, in the northern part of the territory, another hotbed of the order, and equally as far removed from outside influence, they carry out their terrible practice of self-torture. On Good Friday of each year the cañons of the sky-reaching mountains in the vicinity of these places ring with the fiendish cries and weird songs which form part of the appalling ceremony, in the carrying out of which the people seek to do penance for the year's crimes, and start anew.

In solemn procession from the little towns, in the still, cold, early morning, they move slowly along the snow-covered ground, with bare feet and partly uncovered bodies, to the clearing in the cañon, where one of the order, having been previously chosen to the honored position, is crucified on the heavy wooden cross he has carried to the spot on his bare and bleeding

OVER THE TRAIL

shoulders. Others carry rawhide whips, and at every step they lash themselves until the snow-covered ground beneath their feet is streaked red with human blood.

Not many years ago the victim was fastened to the cross with heavy iron spikes, driven through the palms of the hands; and there are many old men in the community to-day with deep indentations in their hands which have only partially healed. The crucified of this generation, however, are tied with rope to the cross, which is less painful, though, in some cases, it cuts through the flesh to the bone before the victim is cut down from the structure.

Leaving Mount Taylor, we ascended the great Continental Divide, which, at this point, forms the watershed between the Rio Grande and the Colorado River. West of the divide is the famous rock formation, with its weather-formed spires of sandstone, called the Navajo Church. This is, in all probability, the only church the Navajos have ever attended; for, unlike the Pueblo Indians, who have partially adopted the religion of the early Spanish settlers in the country, the Navajos have been pagans from time immemorial—the Medicine Lodge, not the church, being the place where their religious ceremonies are enacted.

IV

On the Reservation

IV

On the Reservation

Gallup.—Gold Excitement.—Captain Que-su-la.—Old Fort Defiance.—Government School.—Navajo Hogan.—Trading Post.—Camp in the Heavy Timber.—Navajo Life.

A FEW miles west of the church lies Gallup, an enterprising little American town on the Atlantic and Pacific Railroad. The principal industry of the people of Gallup is mining the soft coal that crops out on the hillsides for miles around. Much of this coal is shipped from the railroad station—the most prominent building in the town—farther west, to California.

At the time of our arrival in Gallup the little town

seemed in an unusual state of excitement, as the possibilities for suddenly becoming rich were discussed by young and old. Gold was the theme on all sides— gold in the Navajo country—and townspeople and Indians were equally excited over the outcome of the much-debated question.

It seems the presence of gold in the Carriso Mountains, in the northern part of the reservation, has been known for years; but, until recently, the Indians have never allowed prospectors to enter. At this time, however, through some of the Senators at Washington, a tract in the mountains had been leased from the Navajos, and work was about to be carried on. Nuggets, claimed to have been brought from the Carrisos, were exhibited throughout the town; but whether they had been found in the tracts leased from the Indians, or been brought from the Cochiti district, or the famous Cripple Creek region—so appropriately named on account of the number of financial cripples it has produced —is hard to tell. The greatest possible secrecy seemed to be maintained concerning the treasure-land. Several claimed to know where the metal could be found in large quantities; but, in many cases, their fear of the Indians seemed to be greater than their love for fortune.

AT CABEZON

On the Reservation

Parties were all the while making preparations to start for " Aladdin's Cave " as soon as word was received from the mountains. Freighters were holding their heavy teams in readiness to carry provisions to the prospective mining camps; expecting to return over the hot, sandy plains and rough mountain roads to Gallup, heavily laden with ore.

The Indians about the town inquired of the stranger, starting for the reservation, whether he was "gold man" or not, with a view to ascertaining the numbers about to be transported to the treasure section.

Why these gold mines, which, at their best, only form a good medium of exchange for the capitalist and land speculators, should cause so much excitement, is merely conjecture, as every dollar's worth of gold taken out of the mountains in the surrounding country has cost ten ; but, as in all such cases, the gold excitement seemed to have turned the heads of the whole community.

In addition to Gallup's several stores, which denote a prosperous town, is the Trading Post, where Navajo goods of every description and variety are seen, having been brought in from all parts of the reservation by the Indians, who think nothing of a three or four days' trip to town, on their ponies, and home again, with the provisions and trinkets they have received in exchange for their goods.

The barrooms of the hotels contain the familiar faro, roulette, and sweat layouts, so characteristic of the Western saloon; but, in spite of these varied amusements, one misses the all-absorbing keno, which affords so much pleasure to the cosmopolitan gatherings in the larger resorts of the Southwest. These games seem to fill a necessary place with the miners and cattlemen who come to town, now and then, to paint it red; but when, at the end of their sprees on regular Arizona tanglefoot, they are pulled together by their friends and started on their homeward journeys, they wake to realize that they—not the town—have been painted.

The four little churches, with a fifth in the course of construction, show the progress the people are making in spiritual work. There are, however, many people in town who do not look favorably upon Christianity, which was quite evident from an incident which occurred on the main street one Sunday afternoon, when two missionaries—one a tall man, with a full beard reaching to his belt, the other a short, smooth-faced man—attempted to hold services before a group of miners. After a short sermon, followed by a hymn

MENDING HIS SHIRT

of the Moody and Sankey type, in which the leaders were the only participants, both knelt to pray, when some one in the crowd threw a package of lighted fire-crackers around them, and, in the racket which followed, a large Newfoundland dog was set upon them. Things growing a little too hot, they no doubt thought it time to seek a more fertile field for their operations, and left in disgust.

The large, well-lighted, roomy, brick school-house on the hillside, where a corps of five teachers work diligently with the children under their care, would do justice to a town five times its size, and is certainly a credit to the community.

On the outskirts of the town is the calaboose, or jail, which is ruled over by the single town marshal, whose duties, by the way, are not very arduous.

Another building of interest in the town is the courthouse, which is just large enough to accommodate the judge, attorneys, witnesses, and prisoners; while the interested spectators catch a word and a glimpse of the proceedings now and then while crowding around the door, outside.

The six-shooter is as yet the only fire alarm in the place; but when emptied into the air at midnight it acts with great efficiency in arousing the people throughout the valley, who rush to the scene of the fire, with buckets in hand, to aid in extinguishing the flames.

The trading store, the general hanging-out place of the Indians for miles around, is a most interesting place. Groups of men and women stand around the store at all hours of the day; those having articles to dispose of dealing with the trader, who gives of his stock of groceries, shawls, calicoes, and cheap blankets of Eastern manufacture, for the blankets, skins, and wool of the Navajos. A squaw who has brought in some blankets and two or three sheep and goat skins from the reservation will step up and offer them to the trader, who, in turn, weighs out some sugar, puts in a package of coffee, takes down from the shelf a roll of calico, and, tearing off as much as she wants, gives them to her. He then tells her, in Navajo, that is the end of his hospitality, and, turning to his assistant, says: " I will hand her over to you; there are forty-five cents due her yet." The assistant finishes the deal by throwing in some trinkets. The squaw, feeling well satisfied with the trade, takes up her belongings, wraps them in her shawl, and saunters

COOKING SUPPER

out of the store with an air of happiness—not so apparent on the faces of the Indians looking on.

At the store is Jim, a good old soul of sixty summers, who knows everybody for miles around; knows their characteristics, habits, and family history; remembers every horse, mule, or cow with which he has ever come in contact. He is an old campaigner, having been in many fights with the Indians; ranging in his time from the Powder River, on the north, to the Rio Grande on the south. He was in the Republican River district in the sixties, when the Sioux nearly exterminated the Pawnees, their meetings having been occasioned by the warriors of each tribe endeavoring to supply their camps with buffalo meat and hides; at which times the Sioux generally returned with an abundant supply of Pawnee scalps in addition to their meat supply. He has served in Uncle Sam's army, in Gen. R. S. MacKenzie's command, on the Powder River, when he fought Dull Knife and his detachment of Northern Cheyennes, and when it was nip-and-tuck as to which would win. He was present also when Red Cloud and his band were rounded up, and when Crazy Horse was brought to terms. Later, he was in campaigns against the Comanches and the

Over the Great Navajo Trail

Southern Cheyennes, who had followed the herds of buffalo into the staked plains. He ended his career with the army in the Geronimo campaign in southern Arizona. He has been rich time and time again from many mining schemes in which he has been interested, but has dropped his money through his love for the old canteen. He has come in contact with many Navajos in his day; but, for some reason, has never learned their language, being satisfied with that of his adoption, abundantly tinged with the brogue of his native isle of the shamrock. There were several visitors in Gallup at this time, among whom were a middle-aged man and his son, who had a camp at the southwestern edge of the town. At a butcher shop up the street they were trying to make a trade for a few head of cattle. Jim said they were Mormons, of whom there were quite a few in town, "and," he added, "the only thing they know is horse, hog, and cow."

Among the frequenters of the trading store was Captain Que-su-la, chief of the Hualapai Indians, of northern Arizona, whence he had lately come. He had arrived at Gallup on his way to Fort Defiance, thirty miles beyond, where he was going to visit

COURTHOUSE AT GALLUP, N. M.

a Navajo friend, whom he had not seen for years; and he was on the lookout for a party about to start out in that direction with an outfit. As our road into the reservation ran through Fort Defiance, we offered the big chief a seat on our bale of hay in the back of the wagon, and started out of town with this latest addition to our party.

Our departure was witnessed only by one or two miners, on their way to work in the early morning, plodding along to join the morning shift without interest in anything else.

Que-su-la, who could speak a little English, proved a most interesting companion, and related in Indian dialect many of the experiences that made up his eventful career. So enthusiastic was the recital of his adventures, that we were, for the time being, transported to southern Arizona, where the Mojave Apaches were burning ranches and running off the stock of the settlers, besides fighting the troops of General McCook, whose scouts were under Que-su-la's command. He told of many narrow escapes and losses of horses and men. Things, however, had been evened up, when occasion permitted, by the killing of the renegades—men, women and children; taking their guns and ammunition; burning their rude shelters and belongings; and, finally, driving those remaining across the border into Mexico. When asked how many Apaches there were, the captain answered, with his characteristic quickness: "How many? Too many."

On our way over the rolling upland toward the mountains, we could see, far in the distance, a column of sand majestically travelling for miles along the dry prairie. It reached perpendicularly into the sky fully five hundred feet, its diameter nearly uniform, until near the top, where it spread out like a toadstool. It slowly passed along, hissing and whirling in its course, crossing the road not far from the wagon, and passing on in the distance until it resembled a mere gray thread reaching far into the clear blue sky.

After camping for dinner, we entered Gaudy's Cañon, where there are many pinnacles and needles of odd forms and design. The high winds, when filled with sand picked up in their course over the prairie, have the action of a natural sand-blast, and have cut the cliffs into caves and avenues, many of which are connected by large holes in the high walls that form their sides. These wind-rocks, as they are called, appear from a distance to have been cut out by the hand

SOFT-COAL SHAFT

of man ; but their beauty, and the grand scale on which they are constructed, show, on closer inspection, that only the forces of nature, with unlimited time, could produce such wonderful transformations.

At sunset, from the top of the last divide, appeared part of the settlement of old Fort Defiance, situated in the little basin north of Cañon Bonito. High ledges of rock form the sides of the basin, and protect the houses from the winds that come up without warning and sweep the prairie sand in all directions.

At Fort Defiance is the Navajo Agency, which is under the supervision of Major Constant Williams, or "The Little Major," as he is called, who looks after the welfare of the Navajos with untiring zeal, and is, in turn, regarded by them with great esteem.

At the Government school, a large three-story stone structure, the Navajo children are taught—the boys farming, the girls housekeeping and dressmaking, and both a fair knowledge of English. Under the care of faithful and diligent schoolma'ams, who supply them with warm clothing and look after them generally, the Indian children live at the agency, amid changed surroundings, and under different influences. Changed in appearance they certainly are, with their hair, the Indian's pride, cut short; and when they are dressed in the regulation school costume one can hardly detect in the uniform-appearing crowd the individuality that characterizes each child on his reservation.

Our camp at Fort Defiance was in the field north of the settlement; and as Que-su-la's friend had gone on a trip into the reservation, he remained with us in camp, where he made himself generally useful. Many a Navajo, on his way from the reservation to the agency, was attracted to the wagon, where he was welcomed by Sam, who explained the details of our trip and gave him further information which, unfortunately, we could not understand. Que-su-la, too, welcomed the strangers, and, although he could not speak Navajo, he gave them, in the wonderful sign language, which all Indians seem to understand, the information that they awaited concerning himself. With a serious look on his face he would open the conversation. Swinging his arm from the west to where he sat meant that he had come over the mountains from that direction; pointing to the ground, then to the moon, and holding up two fingers, conveyed the idea that he would remain in Defiance two months; then swinging his arm horizontally toward the west and

CAPTAIN QUE-SU-LA

(CHIEF OF THE HUALAPAI INDIANS)

pointing to the ground meant he would return to his people at the end of that time. Often during the following three days he went through these explanations to curious visitors, who solemnly watched the chief tell his story, and, in turn, told him of themselves. At the end of these conversations the Indians would turn in their saddles, dig their ponies with their heels, and ride off to the little store in the centre of the settlement.

This store seemed a very attractive place to the Indians, as they formed themselves into groups around the door. The older ones sat there apparently waiting for something out of the ordinary to turn up, and on the lookout for some young buck to ride in from the mountains with blankets and skins to sell, when they would take him, with his lately-acquired money, behind the store building in the shade and start a quiet game of koon-kan, a game of cards the Indian has learned from his Mexican neighbors. Sometimes groups of as many as thirty-five or forty will stand about, expectantly watching the players, ready to laugh at the one whose luck has turned. Some of these by-standers become so interested that they reach over the players, who sit on a blanket on which the cards are placed, and, taking silver buttons from their moccasins, or earrings from their ears, throw them on the cards, which are then covered by their value in money, or by articles of equal worth. Anything a man may possess is liable to be put on a card—from beads, knives, or buttons, to blankets and horses, the latter representing five dollars a head. When the financial standing of the group is reduced to a degree where matches furnish the stakes, the game goes on with as great energy and zeal as if the players' lives were at stake. The Indians find in koon-kan a fascinating amusement, where, as a rule, more time than money is lost; and as the former is of little value to those who join in this pastime, no one seems much worse off for indulging in its delights.

Around the koon-kan group at the store, eagerly watching the game, were two or three uniformed Indian police, who were as interested in the outcome as were the less important spectators beside them. These policemen assist the agent in adjusting differences that arise on the reservation, and see that the Navajos do not drink too much whiskey, which is made in the mountains far to the north.

Next morning, as we stopped at the store before leaving Fort Defiance, one of the men of the town

KOON-KAN

stepped up and asked where we were going, and for what. "Into the reservation," I replied; "I am going to write up the Navajos." "How long will your trip last?" said he. "About a month or so," I told him. "Why," he replied, "I've lived around here for six years, and I've never seen anything worth writing about yet."

Our stay at Defiance ended with a good-by from Que-su-la, who, after helping load the wagon, stood watching us pull out of the little basin and start on the road toward the Carrisos.

We rounded the southern end of Red Lake, where, under the direction of the Government, some work on an irrigating dam has been done for the purpose of storing water in sufficient quantities to enable the Indians to make a livelihood without wandering off the reservation in search of a grazing land for their flocks and herds.

The journey from Defiance northward was, most of the way, an ascent over the Hogback into a beautiful, mountainous country, with big timber, clear springs, and running streams.

From time to time we passed little huts, or hogans, as these Navajo dwellings are called. The most common form of hogan is a circular dwelling made of logs of about equal length, which have been placed on end, like the frustum of a cone. The openings between the logs are plastered with earth to keep out the rain, which, in this mountainous country, is almost a daily occurrence. At the top of the building is a square smoke-hole, directly under which, on the hard-baked ground, the Indian builds his fire. There are no windows in these Navajo homes; so that, with the exception of a small doorway which is generally covered with a much weatherbeaten blanket, the smoke-hole is the only means of ventilation. There are two other forms of hogan, but not so common—one of flat stones, the other of logs. Each is cylindrical in form, with a door in the side, and a flat roof with a smoke-hole in the centre. The summer house of the Navajo, which is occupied only in warm weather, is merely a rude shelter of branches with an opening to the east.

Our passing was always the signal for the members of these households to run to the roadside and see our outfit go by. At some houses we dismounted and went in through the tiny doorways, which were sometimes so low that we had to stoop in order to get into the houses. The Indians would then proudly exhibit

A SHAVE IN CAMP

their treasures to us. Blankets that had been made from time to time, and carefully wrapped up in pieces of old muslin, were brought out from behind the beds of sheepskin that lined the walls of the huts. In little bags kept in some inner recess, or hiding-place, silver ornaments and trinkets were stored away, to be brought out and worn on festal occasions, or to be sold to traders in times of need. We bought several of these trinkets, and left the Indians smiling and happy in the possession of some coins, which, in time, they no doubt carried to one of the "silver men" of the tribe, and had other ornaments made to replace those they had sold to the white man and the "white man's squaw," as they called the Señora.

Toward sunset we came upon a log cabin in one of the clearings. The place was surrounded by Indians, who were leaning against the sides of the house; some with bags of flour and packages of coffee beside them, while several were eating, with apparent relish, sticks of candy, like so many children around a confectioner's shop. The place proved to be a trading post, and the trader and his assistant, a boy who seemed to speak Navajo fluently, were doing a rushing business. Indians on their ponies—men and women—could be seen coming from all directions, with bundles of bright-colored blankets and skins tied on behind them. Sam apparently knew them all; and we could but wonder at his unusually large circle of friends. It seems, however, that, among Indians, everybody knows everybody else, and two meeting for the first time will converse and travel together as though old friends. This utter absence of conventionality is to the highest degree refreshing, and a decided contrast to the ways of the civilized world, where society has reached such an artificial state that sincerity seems a lacking factor in its make-up. We added a few articles to our store of provisions, and climbed into the wagon; while Sam, loath to leave the fascinations of the trading post, swung into his saddle, and we started up the mountain side in the wake of some "gold men," who were on their way to join the prospectors in the Carrisos.

Up the steep mountain road we slowly jogged, until the trading post grew small in the distance, and the Indians surrounding it were distinguishable only by the bright colors of the blankets they wore. We went but a few miles further when sunset overtook us, and we camped for the night under the sheltering branches of an immense pine growing by the roadside;

THE HOGAN

with a clear, cool stream gurgling on its way down the mountain, and a sparkling spring bubbling up on the other side of the road—an ideal camp, with shade and water in profusion! Any one who has camped in the lower country, on the sandy plains, where the wagon forms the only shelter within miles from the burning rays of the sun, and the alkali water of the streams but poorly quenches the thirst of the wayfarer, can appreciate with what a feeling of contentment we pitched our tent in this mountain fastness, and were lulled to sleep by the breeze murmuring through the lofty pine-tops, and the water rushing over its pebbly bed down the mountainside.

The road from here on was alternately up hill and down the sides of deep gulches—so steep that on reaching the bottom of one the wagon-body was lifted from the truck, and had to be unloaded and put back in place before proceeding further.

At the top of the mountain, in a broad clearing, we met a troop of cavalry that had camped there for the night. They were returning from the Carrisos, where they had been guarding the northern trails leading into the reservation, to prevent parties entering the gold region from that direction. Their mission,

however, seemed to have ended in nothing more than
an outing, and they were returning to the uneventful
and monotonous life of a military reservation. Many
of the boys regretted that there was not active duty
to perform ; while the chief regret of others seemed
to be in leaving beautiful mountain camps for life in
the barracks—a life so uneventful as to be hardly en-
durable save for the hope that an outbreak among
some of the neighboring tribes might soon occur, when
they could follow the trail of the renegades and, after
a hot chase, work their carbines to their hearts'
content.

We left the park and the troop, to descend the
northeastern slope of the mountains, over a rocky road
through steep passes, with high ledges of rock rising
perpendicularly on either side of the cañon, where,
down in the bottom of the abyss, lay fallen trees, the
victims of lightning and high winds. The scenery was
so beautiful, so wildly picturesque, as to be utterly
beyond description. Farther on, we met a second
troop of cavalry, fortunately in a clearing, where there
was room to pass. They were about to join the first
troop in camp. The presence of these soldiers, who,
but a short time ago, were prepared to guard the

NAVAJO POLICEMAN

reservation against an influx of prospectors from Colorado and Utah, caused the Navajos throughout the country to supply themselves with cartridges for their Winchesters and for the six-shooters they always carry; and they were ready to go on the warpath at the firing of the first shot. Many an Indian, joining us in camp or on the road, would ask for cartridges, for which they were willing to trade everything they possessed, except their guns.

The road soon descended in a steep grade, and, before we realized the situation, we were wedged in a narrow passage, with a steep ledge on one side and high rocks on the other, so close to the wagon that a person could hardly pass. At the same time, the pack-train of mules belonging to the troops we had just passed approached. We could move neither backward nor forward. The big, heavily-packed mules were corralled, and the jam became each second tighter and tighter as those in the rear closed in on the leaders and pushed them against the team. Finally, one of the mules, seemingly aware of the danger, pressed out of the bunch, jumped up, and climbed over the rocks, almost over our outfit, thus freeing himself. The others followed, one by one, scrambling over the rocks, their hoofs scraping at every step, as they sought to gain a footing on the almost perpendicular slope. One misstep, one slip of a hoof, would have landed one of these beasts, with his heavy pack, on top of our outfit, leaving a splintered mess of the wagon and ponies as material for newspaper correspondents to weave an elaborate account of a horrible massacre among the Navajos.

In a small clearing on the mountainside, a scene of homelike peace and happiness met our gaze long before we reached the spot. In the distance was a little hogan, with bright-colored moving forms before the door, touched by the last rays of the low-descending sun. Beyond was a flock of sheep and goats, approaching, apparently, in a solid, moving mass—not a single outline discernible until they neared the corral back of the hogan, where they were driven in for the night by two little Indian girls, who seemed almost too small for the long tramp they had just taken over the hills to drive the flock home.

In front of the hut, before a crudely-made loom, sat a squaw weaving a blanket of bright-colored wool, while by her side, on the ground, was a young girl with a spindle, getting the yarn ready to pass on

NAVAJO BOYS

to the blanket-weaver. Children of all sizes ran in and out of the hogan, until we could but wonder at the sheltering power of this one small house with its one small room, which seemed very much like the proverbial shoe in which the old woman housed her many children.

We joined the little family, or large one I should say, as they continued their work; while the little ones played contentedly around the door, the laughter of the children harmoniously mingling with the cooing of the babies, who, in papoose cradles, were leaning against the sides of the hogan without even their chubby fists, which were tightly bound down at their sides, to play with.

The Indian baby is a wonder, and is as deserving of special mention as are his parents, who, by reason of their simple, wholesome, and happy lives, are spared the longings for the unattainable, and the dissatisfaction arising therefrom, of which their brethren of the civilized world are constantly the victims. Happy is the Indian who, at the end of the day, can sit by his little camp-fire, surrounded by his children, and eat his simple but satisfying meal. No thought or anxiety for the morrow ruffles the serenity of his happy present.

He lives now. It is always now with him, instead of to-morrow as with us; and as he contentedly sips his cup of present happiness, there are no dregs of future longings to mar his enjoyment thereof.

It is no wonder, then, that children of these parents partake of their nature. From the time the little one is born until he goes with his favorite steed to join his departed brethren in the happy hunting-ground, his life is a joyous one; and in all my travels I have never heard one of these little Indians cry, except when in pain. The captivity of the papoose cradle, in which they remain until old enough to sit or crawl around on the ground, seems unconsciously to school the little ones against being troublesome in after life. Figuratively speaking, the Navajo is born in the saddle. His knowledge of horse life begins very early, and the step from the cradle to the saddle is a short one. First a ride on the mother's lap at a very early age; then he is promoted to a seat behind her upon the horse, where his remaining on the animal depends on holding to the mother, who seems to feel no anxiety, as they jog along the rough roads, that the child may lose his grip and fall off. The fact is, the little one returns from the outing better and stronger, and one

GETTING READY TO MOVE

step nearer that supreme moment when he shall swing himself into his own saddle and ride off alone.

The mental development and training of the child are derived from his keen sense of observation and natural instinct from the time he crawls around the hogan, playing with his pet prairie dog which he has so cleverly caught out in the mountain clearings, or watching his father make saddles and bridles, until later, when his knowledge of plants is acquired; of the trees, from whose bark, together with certain clays, he derives some of the brilliant dyes that color his blankets and moccasins. When, in later years, he accompanies his father on hunting trips, he shows a great keenness in detecting the trail of the elk, and of the deer that furnishes him with his buckskin; telling by the tracks to within a few hours the time when the game has passed through the woods, to the patch of grass, or to the secluded spring where he has often watered his bunch of cayuses and his herd of sheep and goats. Intuitively he learns to shear the sheep, tan their skins, and make baskets and silver-work. The Indian boy is truly a prodigy, showing a keenness and aptitude that only one tutored by Nature alone could possess. Always contented! Always happy! Such is child-life among the Indians! Would that it were more copied by the too-often spoiled children of civilization!

Sam was at home from the first, going in and out of the hogan with the freedom of an old friend, examining the belongings of the family whom he had never before seen, and incessantly talking with them, sometimes as interpreter for us, but more often on his own account. With Sam's help, together with the sign language, in which I was rapidly becoming quite proficient, a sale was effected. Much to the surprise of the entire assembled family, we negotiated for the loom with the unfinished blanket; the carding implements, which resemble curry-combs; and, lastly, the spindle on which the fine-looking young squaw was spinning the yarn. How they laughed as they disposed of one article after another, getting vastly more for the unfinished blanket than they ever dared to hope it would bring when completed and carried to the trader's. They looked derisively at the Señora, who they thought intended finishing the blanket, for what good a half-made blanket could possibly be was utterly beyond their comprehension. It is needless to say the blanket has never been completed, but hangs, just as it was bought from the Indians, among our other collections, highly prized not only as a curiosity, but on account of the associations connected with its purchase.

After buying a young lamb from the flock in the corral, and filling the keg with fresh water, we said good-by to our friends, who, their industry being for the time broken up, stood idly gazing after us as we proceeded along toward the north just as the sun faded from view.

V

Around Our Camp=Fire

Around Our Camp=Fire

Visitors at Camp.—An Old Navajo Historian.—Trading.—Toward the San Juan.

PULLING the team to one side of the road, under a spreading oak growing beside a mountain stream, we set to work preparing supper. Soon the fire was blazing under the tripod on which the frying-pan rested, waiting for the lamb to be cut. The old coffee-pot was in the coals at one side. As we busied ourselves getting supper, a young Navajo rode up on his pony. He was followed by another, and so on until they formed a circle around the fire, from which the savory odor of frying lamb and boiling coffee floated forth into the nostrils of the hungry crowd, and acted as a magnet for every passing man, woman, and child.

The Indians in the meantime had collected the parts of the lamb we had thrown away (they eat all of a lamb except bones and hide), and had placed them in the hot ashes to cook, each expectantly watching his own piece. The women rested their papoose cradles, in which good-natured babies were bound, mummy-like, against the trees near by; while little ones, a year or two old, ran in and out among the group, waiting, as did the older ones, for their supper. As, one after another, they pulled their pieces from the fire, they blew the ashes from them, and settled down to do justice to the meal. Babies, yet too young to walk alone, clung to great hunks of meat, and were now and then given sips of coffee from their parents' cups. As we sat around the fire, enjoying our supper of fresh meat, a young woman—the one from whom we had bought the weaving paraphernalia—rode up, and, like the others, reined her horse beside the camp. She was returning from the trader's, her horse packed with provisions she had bought with some of the silver we had given her. A happier-looking woman never rode

THE BIG PINE

a horse; and later, as she dug her heels into the animal's side, a custom all Indians follow, she passed on down the hill, her hair waving in the breeze, her arms flopping at every jump of the horse, and with a contented, happy expression on her handsome face.

A finer-looking lot of young women could hardly be found than exist among the Navajos. Comely, well-built girls, strong as oxen and graceful as fawns, are constantly seen throughout the reservation; a puny-looking or sickly one being a rare exception.

One by one the Indians left camp as night drew on—all but an old medicine man, who seemed to like the flavor of our tobacco, which he rolled into cigarettes, one after the other, and smoked with great satisfaction. As it grew darker, Sam piled large pine logs on the fire; and when the Señora had retired to her blanket, we three sat around the fire, and talked and smoked; the flickering light playing over the stern features of old Hash-Ke-e-the-tz-ze (whose name translated is, " The Warrior Stands Up ") as he named over in Navajo, while Sam translated, some of the chiefs who had governed the tribe when the first white man came into the country. There were the three brothers, he said, Black Horse, Blue Horse, and Horse Herder, who together governed the people, appointed the time for the dances, for worshipping in the mountains, and for the hunting expeditions which furnished the Navajos with their winter supply of buffalo meat, which they jerked and stored away for future use. He said that the younger of the brothers, Horse Herder, was more friendly to the pioneers than were the other two, having acted as companion and guide to Colonel Dodge, who was Indian Agent in the sixties, and the first white man of whom the Navajos seem to have any recollection.

Between long-drawn puffs from his cigarette the old man said that Dodge made his appearance at Tse-a-lee, where he issued many articles to the people as a token of friendship and good-will. These advances were, for a while, received with favor by the Indians, until the whites began to come in greater numbers than the Navajos desired. The fine mountain country of the reservation, with its stretches of grass and plenty of water, began to be taken up by the unwelcome visitors; and the result was continual quarrelling, and robbing each other of their stock, and destroying homes. He told of the raiding that was carried on, unmindful of the advice of their chiefs, between the Navajos and their Mexican neighbors; it being the opinion of the Indians

A DESERTED HOGAN

that any property of the Mexicans belonged to them if they wanted it. Dodge called a meeting of the chiefs, and told them to tell the people that the best thing for them to do would be to live peaceably with their white neighbors, who would fight the issue to the end, and finally have the entire control of the country over which they were quarrelling.

The first impression the Navajos had of the whites, who were no match for the Indians in their games or races, was that they could take the intruders upon their backs and run off with them. They soon found such was not the case, however, when the cavalry and infantry came over the trail, camped at Fort Defiance, and began an attack on the Navajos; advancing to the cañon north of Tse-a-lee, and on to Chin-lee, where they were met at night by the Indians, who were armed with little ammunition, their principal weapons being bows and arrows. He said that many of the peaceable Navajos were, at the time, in sympathy with the whites, and looked to the officers to settle the difficulties. And to this day the old and experienced officers of the army are looked up to by the Indians, on which account they are most desirable as Indian agents.

He continued that, after advancing to the cañon, the troops had retreated to the mountains near by, where, after a skirmish with pickets, one Navajo was killed. When discovered next day by the Indians, it was found that in taking his scalp the soldiers had taken skull and all, leaving his brains exposed. The Indians, in scalping, merely cut a small disk about the size of a silver dollar from that part of the scalp containing the longest hair, leaving the skull undisturbed. In this instance, as in many others, the Indians found that the whites could go them one better.

As the old man finished this most interesting historical narrative, which he had treasured up in memory for many years, he stopped to light a fresh cigarette, and solemnly said: "If Navajo go down in the ground, white man follow him; if he go up in the air, white man follow him; so Navajo better behave."

Sam piled more logs on the fire, and the old man settled himself for another conversation. One subject after another was discussed, until that of the surrounding country was broached, when he became greatly animated. Going back to the time when,

THE PROVISION WAGON

according to mythology, the mountains in the Navajo country were made, the old man said, pointing to the east, that Tsĭs-na-dzĭ'-n-i, seen from Fort Wingate, were the first mountains made, and in olden times they were worshipped by the Navajos. Tso'tsĭl, or San Mateo, was the second made. Do-kos-li'd (San Francisco Mountain), to the west, was the third made. To the north the mountains which first have their tops covered with snow, the San Juan Mountains, called by the Navajos Depĕ'ntsa, or the Big Mountain Sheep, were the fourth made. Dsĭl-na'-o-tĭl, the mountain the Navajos used to camp around, and which is plainly seen from Fort Lewis, Colorado, was the fifth ; while close by, to the left, is Tso-li'-hi, the sixth mountain made. East of Wingate, A-kĭ-da-nas-tá-ni, which means double top, was the seventh made.

Continuing in Navajo, and making his exclamations more emphatic by frequent gestures, he mentioned in the numerical order of their completion, the mountains representing the shoulders, ears, nose, and arms of one of the great mythological giants of the country. The picturesque Son-sä-lä Buttes, or two stars lying together, which we had but a few days before passed, were the twelfth made; and the

Tu-ĭn-tsa′, otherwise known as the Tuincha Mountains, on the top of which are lakes, called the mountain's water, were the thirteenth made. Next came the mountains representing the back and the hips of the giant. These are known as the black rocks in a circle, which were worshipped in early days; the ceremonial consisting of sprinkling the pollen of flowers on the turquoise in the mountain; at the same time praying for rain, which, in many cases, came the same day. To the west of these are the Dsĭllĭ-che, or Black Mountains, and, said the old man resignedly, as if preparing himself for the ordeal: "It will take four days to tell all about them." As Sam made this announcement, I concluded, as it was getting toward the small hours of the morning, that we would wait for further information concerning the Black Mountains until the morrow. He could not, however, resist talking a little more, and chatted away for some time longer, until his voice grew weak and his eyes were heavy with sleep.

The fire burned low, and as the last note of the old man's voice died away into silence he rose from the ground and, solemnly nodding a good night, slowly walked toward his hogan, his blanketed form dimly

RETURNING FROM THE CARRISO MOUNTAINS

illumined by the dying embers, until he was lost to sight in the darkness beyond.

The following morning was Sunday, and although it was to be for us a day of rest we were up at dawn. Even at so early an hour, some of our guests of the night before had returned to camp, and were waiting for us to awaken and welcome them with a cup of steaming coffee that Sam had just made. The crackling of the burning sticks, and the low murmur of voices around the tent, soon penetrated the canvas, and called us from a sound, restful sleep back to a knowledge of our surroundings.

After making the coffee, Sam finished his preparations for the day by washing his hair in the stream near by, and, after drying it in the sun, he broke open the leg bones of the lamb, and taking out the marrow, rubbed it in his hair, imparting a glossy appearance to the straight, black locks.

The women, who the night before had appeared barefooted, and clad in a single cotton garment, were decked in their holiday costumes, with ornaments galore. Moccasins and black squaw dresses, which Navajo women wear only on state occasions, such as going to the trader's, were donned in our honor. I have several times seen old women stooped with age, walking over the stony, mountain roads, or on the hot sands of the prairie, where the heat must have nearly blistered their bare feet, stop as they approached the trader's, and slip on their moccasins, which they removed again as soon as the homeward tramp began. The moccasin of the Navajo women is similar to that of the Pueblo, the upper part having a long strip of buckskin, which is wrapped spirally around the limb as far up as the knee.

Instead of cheap calico garments, they wore the black native-woven squaw dresses, with bright-colored borders reaching nearly to the knee. On their necks were many strings of beads: both of shell, which they had obtained by frequent trading of horses and blankets with the Pueblos; and of silver, that had been made from coin by some of the Navajo silver-men. Bracelets, necklaces, and rings of silver adorned the arms and necks of both men and women; and belts made of oval silver disks encircled many a waist.

The gathering was like that of a gala or feast day; not because it was Sunday, for the Navajos know no Sunday; and as for ourselves, had it not been for our diary, we would have been in ignorance concerning

SPINNING YARN

either the day or date—all days being so much alike when travelling, as we were, among a people who take no note of the passage of time, except as one season gives way before the coming of another, and that in a most casual way, without special thought or calculation.

Early in the day a fine-looking young squaw, with her baby on her back, came to camp, and, placing the child on the ground, hastened to pay her respects to the Señora, who was holding quite a reception, and receiving all sorts of attentions from the women of the neighborhood, who seemed to regard her dress and our manner of living as very peculiar. They critically examined her dress, shoes, and hat; and at the end of the inspection they were seemingly better satisfied than ever with their own finery and gewgaws.

When I asked the young woman the sex of her child who was playing around on the ground, she proudly lifted her, while her face beamed with satisfaction, and said: "Atét" (girl). This seemed strange to me, for among Pueblo women, of whom I had made considerable study, the girl is lightly thought of, and the parent is very reluctant about divulging her sex to the inquirer. On the other hand, however, if the Pueblo child be a boy, the mother is more than glad to announce, "mucha-cho." This special liking of girls among the Navajos I found to be owing to the fact that, when about eight years of age, they are usually sold to some young brave for from ten to fifty horses —sometimes more. After the sale is effected, the man allows his future wife to remain with her parents until she is considered old enough to marry; which, unfortunately, is often before she is well established in her teens. After her marriage, the girl's future lies in weaving blankets, performing the household duties for her husband, and in looking out for the welfare of the children, whose coming is always hailed with delight by the happy parents.

The husband of the young woman soon joined his wife and child, and at once became friends with Sam, who initiated him into the pleasantries of our camp life. He inspected the outfit, going over everything; while Sam stood near, with the air of part owner in the concern. When the man caught sight of the water keg in the back of the wagon, he suddenly became thirsty, drinking cup after cup from the keg, preferring it to the clear, cold, spring water running within a few feet of camp. On his recommendation others joined him until the keg was nearly empty, when I began to

WEAVING A BLANKET

perceive the reason it had become so popular. It had held whiskey before we bought it, and had become thoroughly saturated with the liquor, which still imparted a taste to the water that was anything but unpleasant. Not a great while had elapsed when Sam came to me and said: "Say, Shä-don-e"—meaning brother-in-law, a name he always called me, but of which I did not discover the meaning until near the end of the trip—"this fellow sick in his arm and want some whiskey." The man, meanwhile, stroked his right arm with his left hand and pointed to his right hand. I knew that if he had an attack of rheumatism, whiskey was the last thing to prescribe for it, so I told him: "Whiskey no good for that kind of sickness." Sam told the man, who immediately put his hand on his stomach, as if in great pain there. From this, I, of course, concluded that some game was up, and watched the rapid development of his disease with amusement. He had many different affections, and made excuses of all kinds to get some whiskey; but finding it of no use, he gave up in disgust, and after another drink from the water keg he seemed entirely cured.

One after another, Indians sauntered into camp; some laden with blankets, others with baskets and all sorts of their belongings which they wanted us to buy. These articles were spread on the ground by their owners, who showed off their fine points in a way that would do credit to an eastern tradesman. Our camp had become a veritable trading post, and a rushing business was carried on throughout the day. I bought three blankets from as many different squaws, some silver-work from a young girl, and a basket from a fellow who was sitting near, weaving a companion piece to the one I had purchased. These dish-shaped baskets are made of the twigs of the aromatic sumac, with intricate designs of red and black colored strands. The twigs are wound in the form of a helix from centre to periphery. Besides being utilized as receptacles for food, the baskets are brought into use as drums in some of the medicine-lodge ceremonials.

Basket-weaving is little practised among the Navajos other than to weave this dish-shaped form. The Apaches carry on this work to a greater extent than do the Navajos, making baskets of a larger variety and of finer texture; their ingenuity and skill in this branch corresponding closely to that displayed by the Navajos in the blanket-weaving industry.

A Navajo Blanket.

One of the squaws here stepped up and wanted us to buy a blanket; but it was altogether inferior to those we had already purchased, and, in spite of her anxiety to sell it, I did not care to add it to the collection. I noticed on her arm, however, an unusually heavy silver bracelet of fine workmanship and odd design, different from anything we had previously seen. "How much for it?" I asked. "She no sell," said Sam, through whom the negotiations were being carried on. She took it from her arm, however, and allowed us to examine it. It was very heavy, containing, as I have since found out, eight silver dollars. Seeing she was not to be further pressed at present, we turned our attention to something else as she put the bracelet back on her arm; at the same time eying the coins her companions were displaying, as though she would like a few also. Still, she was not quite ready to let the bracelet go.

After dinner, the majority of the Indians having remained in camp, I thought I would get a few pictures, and brought out the kodak, which none of these Indians had ever before seen; consequently, they held none of the superstitious fancies concerning a camera that the Indians around the railroad towns have. Sam told them

I was going to make pictures, and showed them some I had taken on my Pueblo trip the year before. At first they objected, not knowing to what terrible ordeal they might be subjected ; but when I pressed the button and announced that a picture had been taken, they were quite willing, as well as anxious, to go through the painless operation again. When I had taken several pictures, and was about to put the kodak back in its case, there was a general murmur of dissatisfaction among the crowd—each wanted his picture. It was hard for them to realize that, after the button had been pressed and all was over, they could not take the finished picture out of the box ; but as photography had not yet reached that state of development, they were obliged to wait.

Hogans dotted the country, here and there, in all directions from camp ; and leaving the Señora with the outfit, Sam and I started out to visit the people in their homes. From one to another we went, picking up, here and there, something for our collection. Blanket after blanket and silver-work were brought out for our inspection ; but when I passed these over and inquired about buying an Apache bottle-necked water-basket standing beside the fire, the owner looked

THE NORTHEASTERN SLOPE

amazed to think I could possibly want it and not his blankets. But I did want it and left the house with it slung over my arm ; while the Indian, well pleased with the sale, went inside to discuss how he had the best of the white man.

After we had visited several houses, I asked Sam where the woman owning the bracelet lived. He inquired, and we soon found the place, where the woman was sitting before her loom weaving a fine, large blanket. She was hard at work, no doubt making up for the time she had squandered at our camp. I noticed she had removed the bracelet and her finery, and was in ordinary attire, without ornamentation of any sort. Over the fire, and tended by the woman's husband, were three large cans of boiling corn. "He making white man's whiskey," said Sam, to whom this was no new sight. The mixture is boiled for two or three days, then it is strained and laid away in closed jars to ferment, when it is ready to furnish the mountain Navajo with whiskey. The vivid picture with its mountainous surroundings strongly reminded me of the North Carolina moonshiners, who carry on the same practice up in the mountains of that country.

I bought a blanket from the woman, then inquired

about the bracelet. At this she went into the hogan, took it from its hiding-place, and came out with it on her arm. She looked fondly at the bracelet, then at the coins I was offering in exchange for it. Still she was loath to let it go. Her husband, becoming interested, left the fire and joined in the conversation, urging her to sell it. Finally, after carefully weighing the subject on all its points, she slipped the bracelet from her arm and handed it to me. Won over at last! Back to camp we trudged, just in time for supper.

Up with the sun, and on to the northward toward the gold fields in the Carrisos. Down we drove over the northeastern slope of the mountains, the timber gradually changing. The tall pines, mountain mahogany, and oak were replaced by a smaller growth, such as the alder and the shrubs known as the aromatic sumac. Further down the slope the shrubs disappeared, scrub cedar taking their places.

The scene changed, the country became more barren; mounds of lava cropped out in the sand at intervals, giving a darkened aspect to the landscape. The only vegetation in sight was the sage bush, the *Yucca Baccata*—a species of Spanish bayonet—and some scrub cedar. By the roadside we passed a nest of the Caro-

SAM

lina dove, situated at the base of a sage bush, and partially protected by it from the heat of the sun. The nest contained two downy young ones, and was constructed of a few small dry twigs, the bottom of the nest being the warm sand. The parents flew swiftly about from bush to bush in an excited manner as we passed, their wings whistling the clear notes by which this bird is so easily distinguished from all others in the vicinity; and we wondered how long it would be before the plump young ones would serve as a meal for some wandering coyote.

As we neared the foot of the mountain, the vast plain between us and the San Juan valley stretched like a great sea shimmering in the sunlight. Far out in this ocean of sand, like monuments of the ages, stood side by side the great needle-shaped formations of stone, Mounts Bennet and Ford.

The utter disinterest of the prospectors from Utah and Colorado, and the return over the plain of many of those from the south, brought our wild-goose chase to the gold region, as well as theirs, to a close; and, turning our backs on the "hoards of wealth," we retraced our steps through the pass through which we had just come.

VII

In the Hogan

VI

In the Hogan

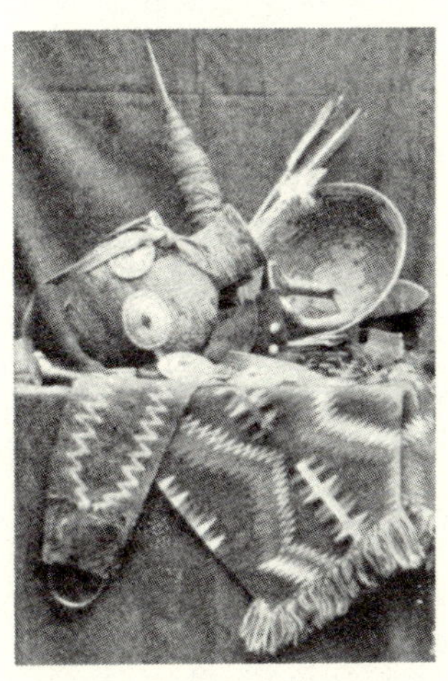

SEVERAL days later, returning to one of our previous camps under the tall pine, we were sheltered from a heavy rain ; and as the lightning played savagely among the mountains around us, Sam exclaimed, "Idni !" and in explanation said : " He's the god of thunder, and is punishing the people of the earth for some wrong they have done." As the flashes became more vivid, we thought it better to move from under our tall protector to the next clearing.

To cut off several miles of road, we started over the

rough country toward Tse-a-lee. Following an ill-defined trail, we reached the bottom of a deep arroyo, where the sand was so soft that the team had all they could do to pull the heavily-loaded wagon along; and as the sides of the arroyo became steeper and the water in the bottom deeper from the incessant rains up in the cañon, it seemed that the sooner we made preparations to get out of the trap the better. At an opening on ahead, one of the sides of the arroyo sloped off at an angle of about sixty degrees; and working our three horses into service, we jumped out of the wagon and tried to urge them up the sandy incline. About half-way up the hill, the wagon became wedged so tightly in the sand that it was impossible for the horses to make any headway; and even after the wagon had been unloaded they could not move it an inch. Two Navajos here rode up, and, taking in the situation at a glance, offered their assistance.

After working for two hours without any sign of success—the five horses being unable to draw the empty wagon up the hill—we decided to back down and find another opening out of the arroyo. Accordingly, I took one of the ponies and started down the cañon, and about a mile below found a place where the

NEAR WHEATFIELDS CREEK

horses pulled the empty wagon out of the river-bed. Once out of the dilemma, we drove to the point where our luggage lay, and, carrying it up the hill, loaded the wagon on the bank above. The rain, which had been threatening for some time, came down almost in a cloud-burst, putting out the camp-fire and reducing our already late dinner to its simplest form. We had lost about five hours by our endeavor to save ourselves a journey of five miles; thus emphasizing the truth of the old saying: " The longest way 'round is the shortest way home."

Farther on we reached the road to Tse-a-lee, and camped within sight of the picturesque and romantic cliffs of Cañon de Chelly, not many miles from the famous White House cliff pueblo ruin, one of the most interesting relics of cliff architecture to be found in this vast territory of pueblo remains. As night drew on, with the crescent moon in the west about to be hidden below the horizon, where a few straggling stars dimly flickered along the border of dark-blue sky, the clouds overhead again let raindrops fall, making the sultry breath from the southwest a cold, piercing lance, and causing one to long for the heat of the fire, the light of which could be plainly seen coming from the smoke-hole of the large hogan a short distance down the road, through the tall pines. We passed into the hut, through the blanket-curtained doorway, followed by Sam, who, after a few words in Navajo to the occupants, joined, as did we, the circle around the fire, where about a dozen Indians were reclining on elbows, on their beds of sheepskin. Under the smoke-hole burned two or three logs which threw out a flickering, unsteady light; now illumining the dusky faces, then throwing them into deep shadow, as the light subsided, leaving the hut in almost total darkness. An old man, the father of the family, sat with his little grandson between his knees, fondling the child, and stooping now and then to kiss him, as he paused in the conversation. Several young squaws, daughters of the old man, were nursing babies; while older children, tired out at the end of the long day, had succumbed at last, and fallen to sleep.

Most of these little people had on strings of beads, with obsidian arrow heads strung in here and there. I reached over and examined one of the necklaces, and asked the mother: "How much?" "No," she said, hugging the child closer to her; "Chindee!" Chindee is the devil, and she was afraid, if she sold the beads, he would run off with the baby.

SAM AT HOME

In the Hogan

An old woman sat in front of a loom, weaving, in the dim, uncertain light, a blanket of intricate design and of great beauty. The most noted industry of the ʼNavajos, and one that has attained world-wide reputation, is blanket-weaving, the occupation of the women of the tribe. Many people of the East, who are fortunate enough to possess one of these rare and valuable blankets, would be filled with amazement could they have viewed it in the process of its manufacture, on the crudely-made loom, up in a lonely spot on the reservation.

In front of most of the hogans, though sometimes the loom is inside, a pole is suspended horizontally between two trees situated a convenient distance apart. To this pole is lashed another smaller one, below which hangs the upper pole of the loom. The distance between the upper loom-pole and the lower depends on the length of the finished blanket. The warp is wound from upper to lower pole when it is time to be operated on. The weaver then sits on the ground before the loom, with feet curled under her, and begins weaving—always at the bottom, and working upward. As that portion which she can conveniently manage from her seat on the ground is worked in, it is rolled down and weighted, and another section of warp is brought into position for her to manipulate. A small reed is run through the warp, separating the alternate threads. In the striped blankets, the yarn is wound on a small stick and pushed through the warp threads; but in one of zigzag design, where the yarn passes through only a few stitches at a time, the squaw pushes it in with her fingers, puts it in place with a small wooden fork, and firmly presses it down with a thin piece of oak about three feet long and nearly three inches wide. These sticks, a fine specimen of which is before me in my much-prized loom, become highly polished by the constant use they receive.

The old woman kept on with her work, stopping only when the firelight became so dim that it was impossible for her to trace her pattern. Around the walls of the hogan hung the saddles, harness, guns, and the saddlebags of buckskin, elaborately decorated with beads by their Ute makers. This bead embroidery, and that done with the quills of the porcupine, are never attempted by the Navajos, being exclusively the work of the northern tribes, who have

A NAVAJO WEAVER

reached a state of rare perfection in the art. All the decorations for festal occasions were hanging around, as were little medicine-bags, which act as a charm to ward off future disease, and to drive away that of the present. The medicine-bag is made of buckskin, and contains charms, as well as plants and herbs. It is carefully tied up, and out of one end projects a bunch of horsehair—the whole resembling a stuffed animal about the size of a small dog. Like the beads that ward off Chindee, the medicine-bag could not be purchased at any price. The very thought of dispensing with these articles seemed appalling to their owners. Sickness within the hogan, and Chindee hovering around without, lying in wait for them!

In cases where the many charms in which the Navajos believe fail to accomplish the desired healing result, they resort to one of the medicine-men, very important personages, who with rites and ceremonies seek to drive away the dreaded disease. As all sickness is attributed to the working of evil spirits, the spirits must be driven from the victim before relief can come to him. In a case of this kind, the nearest medicine-man is summoned, who puts the

patient through a course of treatment of imposing
ceremony, in the carrying out of which he is often
assisted by three or four chanters who, by their
prayers, seek to sing the evil spirits out of the man.

These ceremonies vary in intensity and degree,
according to the financial standing of the patient,
from the simple ceremony of the medicine-man and
his chanters in the hogan, where the patient is rubbed
and sung over, in order to drive the spirits from him;
to the more elaborate and imposing ceremonies of
the medicine lodge, which often last for several days,
each day's preparation being long and tedious, and end-
ing with a night dance. When these charms fail to
work, and the patient dies, it is thought, although his
spirit has returned to the lower world, that his body is
still infested with Chindee. It is further thought that
any one living in a hogan where death has occurred is
liable to die himself, as the hut is under the power of
Chindee, who will ever after have a controlling influence
over it. The hogan is therefore converted into a tomb.
When the body is dressed in its best attire, and wrapped
in a blanket, it is buried in the centre of the hut, the
grave being dug in the floor, that has become baked
hard by the camp-fires of many years. On the grave,

TSE-A-LEE

which, as a rule, is not very deep, are piled stones.   The smoke-hole in the top is then closed up, and the door barricaded with branches and logs, to keep the coyotes from eating the body; an act that would effectually put an end to the man's existence in the hereafter.

If the deceased be a chief or medicine-man, his favorite pony is led to the door where his master lies buried, and, after being hobbled, is given one stroke of an axe between the eyes, when he falls dead in front of the tomb.   The gathering then repair to the nearest stream, where they wash from head to foot; and, after a drink of coffee, they are considered free from contact with Chindee.   From this it will be seen why the Navajo country is dotted here and there with ruined hogans that were once prosperous homes.

Other burial places are on the mountains, away from the hogans, the graves being piled up with stones in the form of hollow squares; and not far away, as may be seen by arrowheads, pieces of flint of which these are made, and bits of broken pottery, are the deserted camping grounds of bygone ages.

As with all Indians, so are the Navajos full of superstitious ideas and beliefs.   This, however, is not surprising, for, being keen observers, they note with alacrity

the happening of events; and not being logical reason-
ers, if a calamity follow a certain action, that action is
ever afterward associated with evil. In this way, one
thing after another comes to be avoided, until the list
has assumed great proportions.

The Navajos sometimes attribute sickness that has
failed to vanish before the skill of the medicine-man to
witchcraft. Such being the case, the person thought to
be infested with witches is looked upon with distrust by
all with whom he comes in contact, and is sometimes
killed by those who seek to rid the community of the
baneful influence. No one, however, can justly censure
the Navajo, who in his innocence seeks to defend himself and his family from the influence of a great evil,
when it is remembered that the good New England
Fathers, living in a comparatively enlightened age, and
enlisted under the banner of Christianity, carried on the
same direful practice, only more highly intensified by
the horrible tortures to which they subjected their
helpless victims.

Within the hogan were comfort, contentment, and a
warmth of hospitality I have never seen excelled in any
civilized home in our land; and we were loath to leave
its kindly shelter, after our evening's entertainment.

KNITTING IN THE SHADE

In the Hogan

But, owing to the late hour, our thoughts naturally turned toward " home," and through the darkness of the night we groped our way to camp, a short distance down the pine-bordered road—to sleep, to dream, and to hasten off in the dim light of the early morning.

After a rough journey, we reached the road to Tse-a-lee. Through the dense forests of pine, oak, and white birch we passed many black-bear tracks, indicating the presence of these animals in large numbers. The Navajos seldom kill a bear—some superstition holding him sacred, and allowing these picturesque animals to increase rapidly ; and although the mountain lion is hunted vigorously, his skin being utilized in various ways, the skin of the bear is never seen in the hogan, it being considered an ill omen even to touch one.

On a hill overlooking the road is the hut of the " silver-man," as he is known by the people of his clan. He furnishes the Indians with all sorts of ornaments : and probably no other tribe decorate themselves with silver to the extent the Navajos do. The articles turned out by the silver-man are made exclusively of coin, which he melts, and works into bracelets, earrings, rings, buttons, belt disks, bridles, and all sorts of ornaments. Hollow bead necklaces, with large inverted crescents suspended, are deftly made; also finger-rings, some of which are in imitation of those worn by the whites, having pieces of turquoise set in. Earrings, many of which are an eighth of an inch thick, are circular in form, and often carry a hollow silver bead, which, together with the weight of the earring, has torn the lobe of many a wearer's ear. Buttons of all sizes are turned out, and are used for decorating moccasins, leggins, and almost any article of wearing apparel. These buttons are convex in form, and are usually decorated with star-shaped designs.

Sometimes a Navajo will sell for fifteen cents a button that has been made from a silver quarter-dollar—thus knocking off at a great ratio instead of adding interest to his investment.

Like the silversmiths of our own clime, who continually seek to improvise some new trinket or ornament to catch the passing fancy of the purchaser, so does the Navajo smith, who turns out ornaments that for ingenuity of design and skill in workmanship are not rivalled by his civilized contemporary.

Harness decorations—such as bridles, which, with the exception of the bit, are almost entirely of silver

THE COYOTE

plates and circular disks—are extremely unique, as well as being highly ornate; and when a squaw is mounted on her gayly-bedecked horse, clad in her best garments, with ornaments in profusion, who that looks upon this interesting picture can question the contentment displayed on the beaming countenance of this modern Queen of Sheba? Belts made of oval silver disks, strung on a narrow leather thong, are worn by both men and women on special occasions; while armlets of leather, mounted with silver plates, are the exclusive property of the more prominent men of the tribe.

In his little hut sat the silver-man, hard at work before his forge, making a bracelet that was soon to decorate the wrist of some prosperous Navajo. The forge of the silver-man was crude in the extreme, and, considering the limited facilities at his command, we could but wonder at the great skill he displayed in his art. On three or four stone slabs rested the little nest-like receptacle of mud that had become baked into hard clay, in which bits of charcoal were burning. The opening through which the air was being forced from the bellows into the pile of charcoal was a passage of clay that had been moulded on a round stick. The bellows was most crudely constructed; the calfskin folds having been made by contracting the wet skin between wooden hoops with rawhide rope. The bellows is worked by hand, the fulcrum of the lever being the end of the board carrying the valve. This board forms the back of the bellows, its lower end resting in a hole in the hard floor of the hut. The little crucibles in which the man was melting the silver were cup-shaped, their triangular edges forming lips, from which the metal was poured off into a mould cut in a slab of sandstone. From this ingot he hammered the silver into shape on an anvil of stone, and decorated it with a simple punch, an old three-cornered file, and an ordinary knife. With this simple kit, aided by his ingenuity, the Navajo smith works the silver into shape and covers it with decorations, many of which have been handed down from the time when the industry began.

As the man worked at the little bellows, he continually replaced the charcoal in the forge to keep the crucible covered. The coins in the crucible soon became white; then, after a little flux had been added, they turned a cherry red; and when the molten state was reached they were quickly poured off into the mould,

IN THE PINES

and the ingot hammered into a bracelet. I should like to have had a belt ; but when the smith had sketched out on paper the design of a disk, I found it would take a longer time than we could well devote to this vicinity to finish the seven large disks it would take for a belt— so I decided to get a finished one from some Navajo we might meet farther on.

After crossing Wheatfields Creek, we reached a park ; and Sam, who was riding on ahead of the wagon, suddenly pulled up his pony and motioned to me to look on the ground in front of him. There, little disturbed by the wind, were bear tracks. They looked large enough to be silver-tips ; but Sam said : " Black, gone this morning, he go back to-night." Over the hills, into the thick timber we followed the trail, until, losing it in the underbrush, we returned to the wagon to make camp a little farther on, hoping that old Bruin would at nightfall return to his mountain lair over the same course he had taken in the morning.

Among the pines, a short distance from Tse-a-lee, we camped in the shadow of a perpendicular shaft of rock, on the top of which were clusters of pines, clearly visible, but appearing like dwarfs, so high up in the sky. This mountain the Navajos call Tse'-dez-än, meaning

Standing Rock; and it is believed by many that on the top is a magician's lake, the water of which is said to be used by the medicine-men in effecting some of their wonderful cures. The presence of this lake is probably the merest conjecture—a matter of tradition, rather than fact—for it seems impossible that any one, no matter how sure of foot, could scale the almost perpendicular sides of the cliff.

From all appearance, our camp seemed to be in a section of country but sparsely settled; but as the column of smoke from the camp-fire reached above the tree-tops—like the smoke signals of the Apaches and other tribes, by which distant bands are informed of the approach of an enemy—an arrival in the vicinity was signalled from hogan to hogan, and another curious crowd of men, women, and children came in from all directions. They lounged around on the ground, laughing and chatting, seeming to regard us as objects of great curiosity. The young fellows, more agile than the old men, danced around and chanted.

Suddenly the attention of all was turned toward a coyote on a hill not far off. What a chance for a shot! Before I could get my Winchester up, however, one of the fellows fired and crippled the coyote, which fell on

THE SWEAT LODGE

its haunches. That the shot had failed to kill seemed to give the Indians great joy ; for it is thought bad luck will surely come to him who kills a coyote ; and the idea of hitting without killing the animal, before the white man did, seemed to increase their hilarity. They jumped up, singing and laughing, and finally left in a bunch, only two remaining to pull the wounded coyote into camp, so that we, not they, would have the bad luck its presence was sure to bring. As they hastened off, I put the coyote out of misery with a ball from my six-shooter, and the camp was still as night. Why this sudden abandonment? Some catastrophe was probably awaited as the result of the coyote's death ; and before long it was evident something would happen. The temperature suddenly fell from one of summer heat to that of a fall night ; and as the wind came up, the mountains to the east became obscured one after another, as with a mantle of smoke which shrouded each in its turn. A forest fire was my first thought, and I wondered if it would be necessary for us to move on before its awful course. On it came, steadily bearing down upon us, until Standing Rock became fainter and fainter, then faded entirely from view. The evening sun was transformed into a golden ball, and the atmosphere, that a short time ago was so clear, became a mass of flying sand, through which the sun shed a rich, yellow light.

As a heavy rumbling of thunder echoed and rëchoed from mountain to mountain, while the lightning played among the surrounding peaks, Sam said that Idni was filling the lake with medicine. As the flashes became brighter and brighter, and the thunder sounded louder and nearer, we crawled into the tent, nearly drenched by the swiftly-falling raindrops. None too soon did we reach shelter, for the storm broke with all the fury of a mountain hurricane. Now the interior of the tent was bright as day, illumined by the piercing flashes of lightning—then followed a terrible darkness, as of blackest night; while the loudly-cracking thunder, following the flashes in rapid succession, added to the grandeur and awful solemnity of the night.

Slowly the storm subsided, until we could but faintly hear the thunder rumbling on in the distance over the mountains; and as we closed our eyes in sleep, to the music of the falling raindrops, it was with a feeling of thankfulness that we had not incurred the terrible wrath of Idni, the God of Thunder.

VII

To Round Rock

VIII

To Round Rock

A Mountain Settlement.—Breaking Camp.—The Council House.—Navajo Sweat Lodge.—Crossing a Hot Arizona Desert.—Cow Meat.—Round Rock Trading Post.

ABOUT a mile up the gulch, to the northeast, was quite a Navajo settlement, the little clusters of hogans being more numerous, and nearer together, than at any of our previous camps. There was also more hustle and bustle among the Indians, which gave the place quite an air of industry and prosperity. Sheltered by the willows in front of their homes, squaws were at work at their looms, weaving with the native wool that others were preparing for them near by. This preparation was going on in all its stages, from the time the sheep were sheared until the wool was spun and handed over to the blanket-weavers. After the wool had been thoroughly washed, it was thrown into large kettles containing dyes of bright yellow, red, blue, and black, and boiled. When the wool had absorbed the dye in sufficient quantity, it was taken from the kettle, spread out to dry, and spun into yarn.

The Navajos make the yellow, red, and black dyes which they use. The yellow is from the flowering tops of *Bigelovia Graveolens*, with a little native alum. The black is a concoction made from the leaves and twigs of the aromatic sumac, a native yellow ochre, and the gum of the piñon, a nut-bearing species of pine. The blue is made from indigo, which the Indians obtain from the traders. The brilliant red was first obtained from a scarlet cloth called Bayeta, originally imported from Mexico. The orange they get from the roots of a sorrel; the green from a mixture of yellow and blue; while the white and black wool—also gray, a mixture of the former—is the wool in its natural state.

The men, too, were not idle, being at work at pursuits of their own—tanning skins, knitting leggins,

WAITING FOR A COYOTE

and making moccasins—or mock-skins, as Sam called them. I inquired of a young fellow who seemed quite an adept at the art if he would make a pair of moccasins for me. He was quite willing, and, as he dropped his other work, I prepared to be measured in true Navajo style. The shoemaker first made an outline of my foot, then cut the rawhide sole half an inch larger than the drawing. The hide was then softened by being buried in moist sand, in which condition it was readily moulded to the foot. The uppers he made of buckskin, colored a deep red-brown, or terra-cotta, with native dye. These buckskin uppers he attached to the sole with sinew, which he ran through corresponding holes that had been made with a fine awl. This made an extremely neat job, and is certainly as creditable to the Navajo as are any of his other achievements. When my moccasins were finished, tried on, and pronounced satisfactory in every respect, the man took some silver buttons from the handkerchief that encircled his head and added the finishing touch that contributed greatly to the ornamental appearance of the foot-gear.

The children, meanwhile, were busy at various occupations, and, as before, I could not but note the happiness that falls to their lot. They are naturally well behaved, are never punished—in fact, that time-worn saying, "Spare the rod, and spoil the child," does not seem at all applicable to the Indian, who, without chastisement, develops the natural, easy-going disposition that characterizes Indian child life. A little boy and girl were playing with some toys that they had skilfully made, and they seemed to find more pleasure in these articles of their own handiwork than do our children in the expensive toys from the city stores. There were horses that had been moulded out of clay, with tails and manes of sheep's wool; and lambs, whose identity was readily detected by their resemblance to the original lamb in the flock that the children daily drive to and from the hillside. The minute observations of these children were shown not only in the excellent reproductions of these animals from nature, but by the Navajo saddles and the cinches of calico they had put on the horses. Dolls they had made of sticks and pieces of calico, the bodies being of wood and the clothes of different-colored calicoes. Other children were climbing up the sides of the hogans, playing with a kid that had strayed from the flock on the hillside; throwing a lariat around a good-natured dog, and shooting at marks with their bows and arrows when no birds happened to be in sight.

We took back to camp, in addition to some clay horses, lambs, and a doll, several fat squirrels, some cottontails, and wild doves that we had come across up in the timber—and we spent the rest of the day writing.

In the cold, still night, when awakening to turn over and enjoy the warmth of the thick layer of blankets under us, the canvas overhead appeared like the great dome of the sky; and as I lay sleepily gazing upward into the seeming great space, a cracking sound broke through the stillness of the night, as of the crunching of bones. Was it a coyote, a gray wolf, or had old Bruin found his way to camp in quest of the bones of the rabbits and squirrels we had had for supper? The Winchester was ready for use; but to raise the side canvas of the tent might inform our keen-eyed visitor that he was not the only one in the vicinity awake; so I waited at the door, looking through the crack in the canvas. There was plenty of light to see him if he would only come around by the wagon, but the bones seemed to keep him busy. After a patient wait for him to finish the meal—a wait that seemed hours—he walked straight for the molasses can, in front of my position at the tent door, and there, in the clear moonlight, stood our shaggy guest—a coyote. Before he had time to plunder our provisions, however, he received a ball behind the shoulder, and, with a loud yelp and a bound, he fell dead a few feet away. On hearing the shot and the yelp, his companions in the woods—possibly two or three in number—became fully aroused to the fact that trouble had occurred, and a cry went up that, to un-initiated ears, would appear as if a pack of twenty or thirty were barking and howling, each in a different key, and with as much energy as their powerful throats would permit.

When Sam returned to camp next morning—he had slept at one of the hogans up the gulch—he looked greatly crestfallen. Another dead coyote in camp, surely some bad luck in store for us! With a most dejected look on his face as he sat down to breakfast, he exclaimed: "Navajo no like coyote!"

Our breakfast was shared with two squaws who had come down the trail leading from their homes on the mountainside, where they had left their sleeping babies, laced in their cradles, to be cared for by the other children, and where a breakfast of coffee. cornmeal mush,

CHARLEY WHITE

and lamb awaited their return. They had taken the last opportunity to dispose of a blanket which one had just finished.

When the outfit was ready to move, Sam began his usual preparation for starting—that is, catching his pony and putting the saddle on him. This feat sometimes took an hour or more, and this morning was no exception. The three days' rest, with plenty of good grass and fresh water, had, we might well say, filled the pony as full of the devil as a young Indian pony is capable of holding ; and all his youthful vigor and viciousness were exhibited at once. When, after much exertion, he was finally roped and saddled, and Sam was about to mount, with a buck he bounded off on a run like a young steer. Up over the hill he dashed, dragging Sam, who had held on to the rope, and whose feet ploughed up the sand at every jump. As they neared a tree, Sam braced his feet against the trunk, and stopped so suddenly as to snap the rope in two. The pony, once free, dashed down the hillside into the prairie-dog village just over the knoll, and the occupants went pell-mell into their houses, head first, as if shot from a gun. The pony by this time was almost wild, jumping and bucking far down the road. A young

Navajo boy, who had been watching the performance, spurred his horse, and started out after the runaway. After a hot chase the animal was cornered in the big timber and led back to camp, where he tried to repeat the exhibition. This time, however, there was not so much bucking, as Sam, being on the lookout, choked him down before he could cause further delay.

Down the road we came upon a large council house, resembling a hogan in shape, but being fully six times the size of one. The large, flat, rectangular roof, from which the sides slanted, was supported by a post at each corner, and, like the hogan, there was a smoke-hole in the centre of the roof.

During the cold weather the meetings of the chiefs, or head men of the tribe, are held in these council houses, where all important questions concerning the welfare of the Navajo are discussed. The chiefs among the Navajos are generally those who have become prominent through their prosperity, and from this number is appointed a head chief.

Since the death of Manuelito, in 1893, who, up to that time, was chief of the tribe, and whose judgment at the meetings was sought above all others, there has been no recognized head chief. His nephew, Pesende, although still a young man, already has shown considerable ability at the government meetings, and has been mentioned as the coming man. In all probability, at the next meeting of the chiefs he will be appointed unanimously as Manuelito's successor.

We passed many hogans, with their adjoining patches of Indian corn, which, after the rain has come in sufficient quantities to yield an abundant crop, the Navajo gathers in and gives thanks to the gods by dancing the Yebichy, a ceremony which takes nine days to perform, and which ends with a night dance.

As we left the heavy timber of the mountains, the herds of sheep on the hillsides grew fewer, and the straying ponies—varying in color from white, buckskin, light bay, and piebald, to black—were seen less frequently. The last sign of habitation as we neared the plain was a low hut—one of the Navajo sweat lodges. In appearance the sweat lodge closely resembles a deserted hogan, but on examination it is evident it is the resort of the living rather than of the dead. At the highest point the lodge is not more than four feet from the ground, and it is large enough only for the one person who goes through the sweat-lodge ceremony as a means of cleansing from sickness or some other evil. The preparation for the sweat consists of heating some stones in the fire outside and carrying them into the hut on sticks. When a sufficient number have been placed inside the lodge, the person sits in the centre with the door closed, and, after a vigorous sweat, comes out in the open air and dries himself in the sun. The single opening of the hut—the entrance—faces the east, and during the ceremony it is covered with a blanket.

We were nearing the great barren plain that stretched, desert like, between us and Round Rock. The scrub cedars became fewer, and as we passed the Tuincha Mountains, whose foot-hills form a border of many-colored strata of sandstone, the familiar sage-bush, which seems to find nourishment enough in almost any clime, disappeared, to be supplanted by the *Yucca Baccata*. The fine sand of the plain became hotter and hotter as we plodded along over this arid tract, where the only object to relieve the monotony of the sandy landscape was now and then the carcass of a horse that had wandered too far from the springs and pools.

A cloudless sky, from which the noonday sun shone without interruption on the sands of the prairie! No

GOING TO THE TRADER'S

vegetation, no water—no sign of life, except yonder, where some ravens were holding high carnival over the carcass of a horse that had succumbed to the intense heat of the plains; and by the roadside, where rattlesnakes lay coiled up in the sun, as if they, too, were under his enchanting spell, and could do nothing but sleep in their hot, sandy beds. Bright-hued lizards glided noiselessly around the yucca plants, as if in search of a shelter from the burning rays. No sound broke the awful stillness save that of the wagon-wheels grinding along the sandy road.

At the last spring we had filled our barrel and canteens with water that was so decidedly alkali as to be hardly drinkable, and we were now on the look-out for a pool back in the cañon, a few miles to the north. Farther on, in the distance, were some moving dots, evidently ponies, that were not far from a pool in the cañon. Slinging the canteens over his shoulder, Sam cantered over the prairie in the direction of the pool, while we kept on our course, slowly jogging along the road. From a crest in the sloping prairie, Round Rock, a large sandstone butte, appeared in the west, like a great fish, the eye of which was a hole that had been worn by the high winds and the prairie sands.

When the sun was getting low, Sam appeared on the crest of the hill with three Indians he had met up at the spring. He produced the canteens, that we might have a refreshing drink, but the water in the keg was far preferable to that Sam had taken the long journey over the prairie to procure—it tasted as if cattle had been wallowing in it.

One of Sam's new acquaintances was a medicine-man ; the other two were chanters, who were accompanying him from settlement to settlement, to assist in performing ceremonies and making cures. Sam called the medicine-man Charley—"Charley White," he said in an aside to me. "He like white man, so his name Charley White." In a similar way many of the Navajos have acquired English names. Charley's Navajo name is De-nava-swish-ke-ze, meaning one tooth gone. Sam had come across the trio up at the spring, where they had been dressing some beef cattle—which partially accounted for the poor condition of the water. They produced the "cow meat," as Sam called it, in long, narrow strips, and, for the first time in nearly a month, we enjoyed a good supper of beef. Sitting around the fire in a circle, we each roasted a strip of "cow meat" in the coals, in true Navajo fashion, and

ROUND ROCK TRADING POST

greatly relished the meal that was so entirely unex-
pected.

After supper we turned in for the night; while Sam
and his friends saddled their ponies and started up the
road to the trading post, a few miles farther on toward Round Rock. We had slept for some time, and
it must have been nearly morning when we heard them
returning to camp. Before long they were seated
around the fire which lighted up the tent, smoking and
chanting, their deep, melodious voices vibrating through
the still, clear atmosphere, and imparting to us a feeling of enchantment, as if we had been transported
into dreamland by the power of the magician and his
chanters.

Next morning Sam looked tired—his eyes heavy
from want of sleep—as from under his saddle he took
a fine saddle-blanket and spread it on the ground.
"Did you buy it?" I asked. "No," he answered,
"Koon-kan last night"—his eyes looked it. "How
much you give me for it?" "One dollar," I replied.
"One dollar twenty-five," said Sam. "All right; throw
it in the wagon." "One dollar an' half," Sam then
said; but I refused to go farther, saying if he intended
making another deal I would give him only a dollar.

So, with a smile, he tossed the blanket in with the others, and crawled under the wagon for a short nap before starting for the trading post.

Just before noon we reached the hard-baked bed of the Rio Carriso, on the opposite bank of which stood the trading post. Part of this one-story building is stone, while the other half is made of logs placed perpendicularly side by side. The trading store and the living apartments of the traders were in the stone building; the storehouse in the adjoining wooden structure. The two attendants seemed much surprised to see us, and wondered why we had come so many miles up in the reservation, over a hard, rough country, to visit a little trading post, which to them had lost all its charm, if, indeed, it ever possessed any. The dreary life they were leading, away from civilization, with not another white man within sixty miles in any direction, with no associates but the Indians who were standing around the store, had so changed them that they looked upon people of their own kin as curiosities. They seemed so pleased to see us, and stared at the Señora with such intensity, that we wondered what so interested them. It seems they had not seen a white woman for three years, and then it was at Fort Defiance, where they had

CAYUSES

gone on a visit. To celebrate the event of her presence at the post, the Señora was presented a dozen fresh eggs, which, with the "cow meat," made our dinner— one not often eaten on an Arizona desert.

The proprietor of the post, an industrious half-breed, being down in the reservation, we were offered the use of his room if we cared to remain at the store; but to sleep in a house when a bed in the tent out in the clear prairie air was obtainable, was not to be thought of; so the invitation was declined.

Many Navajos were at the store with their blankets and hides; but when they spied our outfit, their ideas of trading seemed to vanish, and they flocked around the wagon. Among the others was an old medicine-man, bent with age, but bright-eyed, and interested in all that was going on. He climbed upon the wagon, examining everything in turn; and when he uncon-sciously put his hand on the coyote skin that was hang-ing on the back of the wagon, an exclamation from those standing beside him caused him to withdraw it as if he had been bitten by a tarantula. The Indians at once broke into a hearty laugh, guying the man, until, in desperation at their taunts, he broke away and ran to the well down over the bank, where, in a tub, he washed and scrubbed the hand that had come in contact with the coyote skin, as if his only hope of future happiness depended upon a thorough cleansing. For should the influence of the evil spirits that infested the skin fall upon him, what hope had he of anything better than a life of torture?

From Round Rock we had planned to return through the Chin-lee Valley, and visit the ruins of the famous cliff dwellings, known as the White House in Cañon de Chelly; but most of the Navajos had already left the cañon for camps in the mountains, on account of the unusually long drought to which the country had been subjected. For this reason, and also because of the heavy roads, we decided to make Round Rock Trading Post, but twenty miles from the Carrisos, in the heart of the reservation, the terminal point of our journey of two hundred and sixty miles over the Great Navajo Trail.

VIII

The Navajo

VIII

The Navajo

Is the Navajo to be the next victim of the Government's Indian policy? Is the discovery of traces of gold in his scantily fertile land to be the entering wedge of the whites? This would, in the end, result in the negotiation, through the Senators at Washington, for the purchase of the Indian's now insufficient arable land, which is his only hope of existence.

Not many years ago water and grass were plentiful; but as the tribe has increased, so has the demand for water and pasturage, until now the land cannot furnish food enough for the vast flocks and herds. Many thousand Navajos have thus been obliged to wander off the reservation, gradually settling along the streams, as far east as the Rio Puerco; south, as Zuñi; and as far west as the Grand Cañon of the Colorado, intruding on the pasture lands of the Moquis.

This necessitated spread of the tribe is a constant menace to the cattlemen in the vicinity of the reservation; and at present the outlook for either is not the brightest. The land included within the reservation is sufficient in area for their numbers, were it not in many large tracts a barren waste, where there is not wood enough to light a camp-fire.

The Government has attempted to build storage reservoirs, and lay out a system of irrigation which, if completed, would, to a considerable extent, tend to alleviate the wants of these industrious and energetic people; but, after years of labor, the work is still far from completion.

To be sure, the Navajos have committed many depredations, running off stock, and, in some instances, killing the settlers. These quarrels, in most cases, have been over the springs, which in the much-disputed country are scarce.   The deeds, therefore, have been committed out of simple protection, and are exactly what hundreds of whites have done, not only to the stock and settlements of the Indians, but to those of their own race as well, when a bunch of cattle could be gained by so doing.   But where the Indian is concerned, only one side of the story is ever told, and there it ends.   In the few cases where they have beaten the whites, the Indians have in return been defeated by the troops.

The traders and people around the reservation seem to think it strange that the Navajo looks with suspicion upon every white man with whom he comes in contact; but a review of the treatment other tribes have received at the hands of the whites will clear up any misunderstanding on that point.   Time and again the Indians have been driven from their beautiful mountain streams and forests, where game was plentiful, and their wants supplied by their skill in hunting and trapping, to have their picturesque lands taken up by the whites, who seemed to think they had more right to them than did the people whose forefathers had hunted there for generations.   The lands to which they were driven were, in many cases, barren wastes, from which they fought their way back, avowing that it was as well for them to die on the battlefield as to have their people starve to death on the tracts that had been provided for them.

In a report from General Knox, Secretary of War, to President Washington, dated June 15, 1789, it is stated: "The Indians, being the prior occupants, possess the right of the soil. It cannot be taken from them, unless by free consent or by the right of conquest in case of a just war. To dispossess them on any other principle would be a gross violation of the fundamental laws of nature, and of that distributive justice which is the glory of a nation." This thoroughly expresses the sentiment of that time, and it would be well were it the sentiment of the present; but to-day we find the Indian reduced by war after war, treaty after treaty, and purchase after purchase, to such an extent that many tribes have entirely disappeared.

To lease the Navajo lands for mining purposes to reliable persons, who will vacate when the resources become exhausted or when the lease will have expired, would leave the Indian in possession of the land, which would still retain its ability to furnish pasturage; and possibly the development of the streams and springs would tend to increase the fertility of the soil. But would not the contact of the Indians with frequenters of the mining camps be a source of trouble, overbalancing any benefit that might be derived therefrom?

In the event of gold being discovered in sufficient quantities to mine, a boom would be started—the news spreading from gulch to river-bed, thence from town to town; and in a short time the reservation would be entered from all directions by people who, not being so fortunate as the original lessees, would try to reach the treasure section by force. To prevent serious trouble would take a large number of troops. The Navajos, who are well armed, would resist the intrusion to their utmost capacity, and many parties would never reach their destination. It is tax enough on the Navajo to be compelled to eke out an existence in a partially-barren country, without having to resist an invasion of the whites.

To purchase the land, of course, seems just and right; but think what the result would mean to the Indian! The payment made to each, individually, would be so small that he would in a short time be without money or land—the latter having been thrown open to prospectors (many of whom had been run out of other mining camps) and to that class of people who surround Indian reservations with the expectation that at some time the land will be thrown open for their benefit. They will then enter with a rush, taking up the land, which, having been much overrated by their strong imaginations, would soon prove as unable to provide them with the necessities of life as it was the Indians before them ; and, were it not for their weakness for the yellow metal, they would pull up stakes and leave in disgust. Then, when the Indians have received payment for their land, they, with the smattering of knowledge they have received from the schools, will be supposed to earn a livelihood among a people whose business ability is far superior to that of the people who but a short time before were living under the care and protection of the Government. The outcome of this would be a change, after the second generation, from the present full-blooded Navajo to a half-breed, who, as is generally the case, would inherit none of the best qualities of his ancestors on either side.

Unlike the Pueblo Indian, who takes more kindly to the ways of civilization than his roving neighbor, having for centuries lived partially civilized, the Navajo seems unable to withstand any change from the customs he has followed for ages.

Up in the gulches on the mountain-sides—miles from the society of their oppressors—we find the Navajos in their little settlements, which, if carefully observed, would present a different phase of the Indian question to those great reformers who look only on the theoretical side of a question. Without civilization the Navajo has lived and prospered; and that his life on the reservation has proved nothing but beneficial is shown by the rapid increase of this, the largest of the remaining full-blooded tribes.

Why, then, thrust upon a people who have always lived an outdoor life, like children of nature that they are, a state of civilization for which they seem entirely unfit, as well as being strongly opposed to? The Navajos have ever been able to provide for themselves, until suddenly brought up against the ways of civilization, which they can but a short time withstand, and which have endangered their native customs, habits, and industries.

The civilizing experiment has been tried many times, with the result that the tribes so dealt with have been civilized out of existence.

Over the Great Navajo Trail

The Indians, like the few remaining herds of buffalo, are reaching that point where they are in need of the greatest care and protection, in order to save those who remain ; and it is time the Government devised some method whereby they can be freed from the evil influences by which they are constantly surrounded.

Under the policy now in vogue, the lands of the Indian cannot be protected against the encroachment of his more fortunate white neighbors, unless the time comes when that universal law, the survival of the fittest, be laid aside—then, and only then. And should the Fathers at Washington see fit to throw open the Navajo Reservation to the whites, the only place left to transfer the Indians from their present home is to some of the lava-flow sections in the central part of the territory, where there is absolutely nothing on which they can live. They will then make complete the extermination of this once powerful, progressive, and peaceful people —in one or two years, instead of one or two generations as is being done by the present Indian policy.

THE END.